ESSE...
PSYCHOLOGY
General Editor
Peter Herriot

D4

INDIVIDUAL DIFFERENCES

ESSENTIAL

PSYCHOLOGY

INDIVIDUAL DIFFERENCES

Richard Kirby and John Radford

Methuen

First published 1976 by Methuen & Co Ltd
11 New Fetter Lane, London EC4P 4EE
© 1976 Richard Kirby and John Radford
Printed in Great Britain by
Richard Clay (The Chaucer Press), Ltd
Bungay, Suffolk

ISBN (hardback) 0 416 82840 X
ISBN (paperback) 0 416 82850 7

We are grateful to Grant McIntyre of
Open Books Publishing Ltd
for assistance in the preparation of this series

Contents

Acknowledgements

The author and publishers would like to thank the following for permission to reproduce a diagram in the text (for full bibliographic details please see the text):

The American Association for the Advancement of Science for Fig. 12.1

Editor's Introduction

In what ways are individuals unique, and is their uniqueness open to scientific investigation? Richard Kirby and John Radford continue, refreshingly, to disagree on this and other questions which arise in any discussion of persons as individuals. Supposing that people differ along certain common dimensions, what are these dimensions? Is there any justification at all for separating off for analysis such dimensions as intelligence, extraversion, and attitudes, when the whole person is greater than the sum of these parts? Granted that there is, for what reasons do people differ along these dimensions? And is their *behaviour* different because they are different sorts of person, because of the situation, or because some sorts of people behave in certain ways in some situations, others in others? Read on!

Unit D is a crucial part of *Essential Psychology*. Many who are dissatisfied with all current models of man see the concept of man as an individual and social person as the best alternative. This is because it emphasizes the uniqueness of the experience of each individual and also the notion that he acts upon his environment in a purposeful way. The books in this unit all demonstrate how the basic assumptions of personality theory and research are changing. Instead of personality being described in terms of forces driving people from within or events manipulating them from without, individuals are now being described as persons each with his own way of construing reality.

Essential Psychology as a whole is designed to reflect the changing structure and function of psychology. The authors are both academics and professionals, and their aim has been to introduce the most important concepts in their areas to beginning students. They have tried to do so clearly but have not attempted to conceal the fact that concepts that now appear central to their work may soon be peripheral. In other words, they have presented psychology as a developing set of views of man, not as a body of received truth. Readers are not intended to study the whole series in order to 'master the basics'. Rather, since different people may wish to use different theoretical frameworks for their own purposes, the series has been designed so that each title stands on its own. But it is possible that if the reader has read no psychology before, he will enjoy individual books more if he has read the introductions (A1, B1, etc.) to the units to which they belong. Readers of the units concerned with applications of psychology (E, F) may benefit from reading all the introductions.

A word about references in the text to the work of other writers – e.g. (Smith, 1974). These occur where the author feels he must acknowledge by name an important concept or some crucial evidence. The book or article referred to will be listed selectively in the References (which double as Name Index) at the back of the book. The reader is invited to consult these sources if he wishes to explore topics further.

We hope you enjoy psychology.

Peter Herriot

Preface

We wrote our second text in this series in the following manner. First we discussed the issues and decided on a general plan. Then we divided the chapters into two. RK wrote about sixteen of them and sent them to JR who revised them – much in some cases, less in others. The other chapters JR wrote straight off. We discussed JR's version and made some small alterations.

We realized we could not hope to cover the vast topic of individual differences in some 40,000 words. Anastasi's compendium *Differential Psychology*, which after all is only a summary of available research and theory, runs to 664 pages. We have tried to introduce most of the main issues, choosing to do this in a series of quite short sections. Likewise we have tried to introduce the investigators we think most important, giving a brief biography of each of five.

Short as the book is, our time turned out to be even shorter, due to those foreseen and unforeseen circumstances that beset all authors, as Samuel Johnson pointed out in his *Life of Pope*. Johnson wrote *Rasselas* in the evenings of a week; and our admiration for the great lexicographer has never been higher than now.

I
H. J. Eysenck

Professor H. J. Eysenck is perhaps the most famous, at least in Britain, of all the psychologists who have studied the problems of individual differences. This is partly because, unlike earlier scholars, he has had the benefit of television and mass-produced books. It is also because he is perhaps the most prolific of all theorists of individual differences. To date he has published thirty books, and his bibliography for articles and book chapters runs to over five hundred items. In this massive flood of publications this remarkable man has explored in theory, survey, and experiment all the most outstanding problems of individual differences, has offered solutions, and has gathered a voluminous set of rigorously derived data to bear on the problems and the solutions. Among the issues to which Eysenck has contributed are: the nature and structure of personality (see D3); the measurement of personality; its origins; the role of intelligence in the total personality; the relation of personality to mental illness, criminality, sexual propensities, political beliefs (see F3); the analysis of individual differences by sophisticated statistical techniques; the nature and treatment of personality disorders; the nature and origins of differences between races.

For this last, Eysenck has become in some quarters not so much famous as notorious; and has been subjected to abuse, and even physical assault, by individuals of self-proclaimed 'anti-racist' beliefs, whose dogmatism seems matched only by their ignorance. In the confused minds of such persons, angry vilification is the only answer to scientific research with the results of which they happen to disagree. Later, we shall touch on some of the baffling complexities of the racial problem. Among psychologists, and perhaps among the general public, Hans Eysenck is probably best known for three things. First, an uncompromising advocacy of a fully scientific, empirical psychology comprising general laws of human behaviour, tested by experiment and yielding useful predictions. Second, his own major effort in this direction, the establishment of fundamental dimensions of personality, the most famous being 'introversion-extraversion'. Third, the applications of his personality theory, especially to the treatment of disorders of behaviour in the form of 'behaviour therapy' (see A3 and F3) (a term coined by Eysenck). Eysenck's work has become known not only through his massive scholarly output, but through his own brilliantly lucid accounts for the general reader.

There is a single theme which unifies Eysenck's psychological interests: it is the *scientific study of individual differences*. The origins of this endeavour can be traced almost to the beginnings of science itself. The Greek philosopher-scientists of the sixth century BC attempted to determine, by rational inquiry, what were the ultimate constituents of nature, of which man, of course, is a part. From this derived the concept of four main *types* of men, according to the balance of the constituents (humours) within them. The notion has persisted until recent times, and now, indeed, seems to be in many ways consistent with Eysenck's own theories. The greatest of the Greek thinkers, Plato (?427–347 BC) and Aristotle (384–322 BC), both spent much time analysing the puzzling differences between people. The problem of course has likewise preoccupied scores of artists, theologians, and scientists of all kinds, but it was only in the mid-nineteenth century, as it seems to us now, that an actual science of individual differences began to emerge. Among many contributing factors, a particularly important stimulus was Charles Darwin's evolutionary account of the

Origin of Species (1859). Apart from its general impact, this specifically inspired Darwin's cousin Francis Galton (Chapter 3) to investigate the origin of variability in the human race. He began a line of great psychologists working in London: Pearson, Spearman, Burt, Cattell, Vernon; and it is to this line that Eysenck belongs. He was, in fact, a pupil of Sir Cyril Burt (Chapter 11) and a colleague of R. B. Cattell (Chapter 7). As many writers have shown (e.g. Karl Popper, Thomas Kuhn, E. H. Gombrich), intellectual advances emerge from specific contexts of knowledge and thought, and largely consist of adopting and changing what already exists. The study of individual differences is no exception.

Hans Jurgen Eysenck was born in Berlin in 1916. His parents were actors, and from them he learned to appreciate art and literature as well as science. In 1934 he was required to join the Nazi party and become a member of the SS if he was to be allowed to enter the University of Berlin. These conditions were as distasteful to him as the Nazi regime itself, and he left Germany for France, where he studied French literature and history at the University of Dijon, before deciding to settle permanently in England. Eysenck studied English literature and history at the University College of Exeter, and then applied to read physics at University College, London. But the authorities would not recognize his qualifications as suitable for so strictly scientific a study. So, being unable to take a year's qualifying course, he asked if there was any science subject which he could take. 'Oh yes,' they said, 'there is always psychology.' Eysenck said, 'What on earth is psychology?' 'Oh,' they said, 'you'll like it.' And that, Eysenck reports, is how he chose his life's work. Since then, he has been determined to make psychology into a truly scientific subject.

After this decision, Eysenck's career proceeded along more conventional lines. He took his BA and PhD at the University of London, beginning in the way he intended to continue: he published several articles before even taking his first degree and had numerous publications to his credit by the time he took his Doctorate. In the meantime he studied factor analysis with Burt, statistics with Pearson, and psychiatry with Herzberg.

In the Second World War he volunteered for the armed forces, but, being an 'enemy alien', was rejected, and indeed nearly interned. Eventually he was allowed to join the Civil Defence, and worked in Air Raid Precautions. In 1942 he joined the staff of Mill Hill Emergency Hospital as a research psychologist. This began his study of psychopathology and its relation to personality. In 1947 Eysenck was appointed Director of the hospital's psychology department and in 1948 became, in addition, a Reader in Psychology at the University of London.

In 1950 the famous Maudsley Hospital in Peckham, South London, founded an Institute of Psychiatry, and Eysenck was co-founder of the psychology department there. He has since been its director, and, since 1955, Professor of Psychology in the University of London.

Hans Eysenck is now married to Sybille Rostal, who is also a psychologist. He has a son by a previous marriage who is likewise a research psychologist.

Eysenck has many recreations and hobbies, including a fondness for reading the lives of scientists. He does so, he confesses, to see if his personality theories are confirmed in biographies as well as in experiment. But he would be the last to use this information as *scientific* data; that is why it is only a hobby.

2
The problems of individual differences

The existence of individual human beings raises, we argue, two groups of problems for psychologists (see D1). The first group consists of problems of the *differences* between individuals and between sets or classes of individuals. The second group is concerned with the sensation of *individuality* within persons and with the existence of the self. These problems overlap and intermingle in the untidy way that science has; and psychologists have made things more confusing, both for themselves and others, by using labels rather inconsistently to refer to their various investigations. If may be helpful to list here some of the more common uses.

Individual differences is perhaps the most general term, and refers to the study of all the various ways in which individuals can differ from each other relatively permanently. The expression *differential psychology* is sometimes found with more or less the same meaning.

Personality (see D3) sometimes refers to the whole functioning individual, including his intellect, emotions, social behaviour, and so forth; sometimes it is used rather more narrowly, meaning mainly the emotional and motivational side. *Personology* is a word sometimes used to mean the study of personality.

Intellectual abilities is a general term for functions underlying thought and reasoning. Such abilities have probably been

15

the most extensively investigated of the ways in which individuals differ. Many theorists have supposed that there is one primary or fundamental ability important in all such functions, and have used for this the word *intelligence*.

Cognition, conation, and *affect* are three terms with a long usage in psychology, and refer respectively to such activities of the mind or intellect as perceiving (see A4), thinking, language (see A7), memory (see A6); to needs, wishes, drives, motives (see D2); and to feelings or emotions. Another word sometimes used for the first sort of function is *noetic*, while the other two are grouped together as *orectic*. As mentioned, *personality* sometimes refers mainly to the latter.

These words, and many others, are labels that psychologists have attached to such features of their unstable and largely uncharted territory as seem to offer relatively permanent points of reference. Their convenience for purposes of carrying out research, setting examinations, and writing books, should not delude us into thinking that they necessarily correspond to reality. Nor, most importantly, that the phenomena they stand for do not interact. Even if we can, for example, reliably isolate a feature called 'intelligence', and show that measurements based upon it enable us to make useful predictions, it is still obvious that these must depend upon what the individual *wants* to do, on his interests, upbringing, social setting, and a thousand other variables.

Looking back on the short history of psychology, we can see that a number of traditions of inquiry weave in and out, sometimes closely interacting, sometimes in relative isolation. One such tradition is concerned with individual differences, and particularly with their measurement – largely for practical purposes. This endeavour is often labelled *psychometrics*. Other main traditions include philosophical analysis of psychological problems; clinical diagnosis and treatment; and experiment. The experimental tradition, indeed, is often seen as the core or mainstream of psychology proper (see A1). Throughout most of their lives, psychometrics and experiment have interacted rather little. Experimentalists have sought to establish basic facts about human behaviour and experience which in principle would be true for all members of the species. Several authors, notably Eysenck (1966), have argued that in neglecting individual differences, much of the value of the experimental findings is lost.

The origin of research problems

We have said that the existence of individual human beings raises two groups of problems for psychologists. This, however, is an oversimplified way of putting it. To begin with, these two groups are merely what seem to us (your authors) a convenient way of sorting out some of the main issues, though we hope others would agree. More important is the fact that, as far as we can see, the existence of human beings actually generates an infinite number of problems.

Several arguments can be presented to show why this must be so. Let us mention two, which have particular force with regard to psychology, due to the unique position of a science whose exponents are part of its own subject matter. The first is that problems generate other problems. Obviously they do so in a practical sense: no sooner do engineers solve the problem of the internal combustion engine than we are faced with traffic jams and pollution, control of which causes difficulties over individual rights, transport of goods, etc., and so on, apparently for ever. However it has been argued (with notable force by Karl Popper) that this is not just bad luck, but must logically be so. On Popper's view of science, there can never be solutions of whose truth we can be absolutely certain. Science proceeds by formulating the best hypothesis possible in the light of existing knowledge, and then looking for evidence that would refute it. As long as none is found, we can continue to hold the hypothesis. Popper's formula for science is that problems generate theories which lead to criticism which in turn produces further problems, and so on for ever. While there are objections to Popper's thinking (see D1), it is not easy to escape from this particular conclusion. In the case of psychology it has particular force, since every explanation of human behaviour offered by a psychologist is itself an addition

17

to human behaviour, calling for an additional explanation (see F1).

The second line of argument stems from the nature of scientific problems. There is, perhaps, a common conception that science deals, as it were, with a queue of problems, finite in number, existing independently of mankind, and waiting patiently for his attention. But it is not only that the queue would be endless: it is that problems only exist with reference to human beings. Science is only the endeavours of human beings to understand. In this sense *man is the measure of all things*, as Protagoras stated. (Of course, as science fiction fans will point out, there could be non-human scientists too; but the same argument would hold for them.) Now we certainly do not know even all the situations that mankind has found problematic in the past, let alone what may become so in future. Indeed following the first argument, we can never know, since we can never predict the future and *a fortiori* the human future.

While we agree on this, the present authors disagree on how important it is. JR feels that the main task of psychological science is to concentrate on what we have actually got by way of human behaviour and experience, while RK is more impressed by the dangers of assuming that this is a fair sample. We wish to stress, however, that here we are dealing only with our selection from an already arbitrary selection. This is not a mere abstract point. For example, there is every reason to think that our concepts of intelligence are strongly influenced, at the very least, by their having arisen in a Western technological context. These concepts in turn have had enormous effects upon education, virtually throughout the world. Our present selection is mainly of differential psychology *per se*: we have less to say, for example, of personality theories (D3), of the self (D1, F7), or practical applications (E2).

The problems of human variety

One of the most basic functions of the human mind is categorization or sorting. A spontaneous reaction on seeing something for the first time is to allocate it to an already known group. Some readers may recall the opening scene of the *Superman* television programmes of the 1950s. An unidentified flying object hove into view, where upon the crowd searched their categories: 'Is it a bird? Is it a plane? No, it's Superman!' This function is often unconscious. Indeed it can be pointed out that the lower one goes down the phylogenetic scale, that is to say the simpler the organism one is dealing with, the more automatic the function, and the fewer and simpler the categories into which incoming stimuli are classified. A sea anemone, for instance, reacts in terms of 'edible' or 'inedible', whereas humans (some of them anyway) can not only readily distinguish, say, real beer from worthless keg, but can discriminate many subtle varieties of the former. Indeed we can identify unique individuals as the Superman crowd did, as we all do every day, and as human babies do from an early age – at least with their mothers (see C1).

It is more perplexing to know whether science can deal with individuals. Science seeks, in general, to formulate more and more all-embracing theories. In attempting to do this with human beings, we may be losing that which makes them human; and Gordon Allport (Chapter 17), in particular, has decared that individuality raises unique problems for science.

Human beings in general, then, and scientists in particular – though not necessarily for the same reasons – wish to classify the members of their species. Into what categories can we rightly sort the representatives of *homo sapiens*? Evidently they are different from one another: are the differences finite, and if so how many categories are there? Problems of this kind have led to the postulation of human *typologies*, or the statement of a limited number of categories into which every human is supposed to fall. Another sort of answer is that persons vary along *traits*, that is persisting characteristics or dimensions of personality (e.g. dominance, honesty or the like). In practice we employ a limited number of traits, both in common use and for scientific purposes, although there are some thousands of words for them.

Both these answers recognize the common-sense view that

19

there is some stability in at least some aspects of human personality, and that groups of individuals share common characteristics to a greater or less extent. A second sort of problem concerns the ways in which these characteristics are *related* within the individual. Some of the most popular examples involve supposed relationships between bodily and mental characteristics. Is it true that red-headed people have bad tempers, or that fat people are exceptionally affable? Where such relationships have been systematically studied, what usually emerges (as it often does with behaviour) is not an all-or-nothing result but a *correlation:* a tendency for two variables to go together (see A8). This was one of the most useful concepts brought to psychology by Francis Galton (Chapter 3). There are three important points about it. One is that it allows for the notion of *partial causation:* it very often turns out that some aspect of behaviour is partly caused by a particular variable that can be isolated, and partly by others which may or may not be known. Thus we certainly do not know all the variables contributing to the development of intelligence; but we do definitely know that one of them is adequate nutrition. Secondly, correlation forms the basis of factor analysis, the most powerful statistical technique we have for disentangling the complexities of behaviour (see Chapter 4). Thirdly, it must be realized that although correlation *suggests* a cause, it does not *prove* it. Thus the existence of a correlation between smoking and lung cancer does not, by itself, prove that the one causes the other. It merely states that, in the population as a whole, as smoking increases, so does cancer. In the case of any individual, we can say with a particular degree of probability what likelihood there is that if he smokes heavily he will get cancer; or conversely if he has cancer, that he has been a heavy smoker. From this fact alone, the possibility always remains that both phenomena are caused by something else. It is necessary to go further, and find the actual physiological mechanisms involved; what happens to lung tissue when subjected to the constituents of tobacco. When we are dealing with psychological variables, it is often not possible to take this further step.

The third sort of problem concerns the *distribution* of individual differences in the population at large. It is now more or less assumed (but see F8) that any psychological vari-

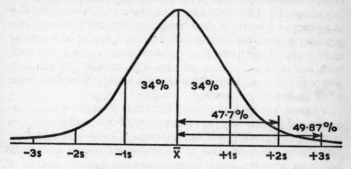

Fig. 2.1 *The 'normal distribution'*

X̄ indicates the *mean* or arithmetic average.

s indicates a *standard deviation*. This is a measure of the spread of the data, such that 68% fall within one standard deviation above and one below the mean.

These two figures can be used to summarize results. Thus if heights of men were measured, they might be summarized (in inches) as M = 67 ± 3. This would mean that the arithmetic average was 5'7''; 68% of men were between 5'4'' and 5'10'; 9·54% between 5'1'' and 6'1''; and so on.

able will tend to be *normally distributed* (Fig. 2.1). This assumption is likewise due to Galton. The concept itself derives from the applications of the mathematics of probability, which were worked out by Gauss (1809). It turns out that these apply to a number of natural phenomena, including human characteristics such as height, as was shown by Quetelet (1835). Galton argued that psychological traits such as intelligence must have a physical basis and, therefore, must also follow the same pattern. And indeed for many characteristics this does seem to work. It is important to realize, though, first that the normal curve is an ideal, a mathematical abstraction. Natural phenomena only *tend* to fit it. Second, there is no logical reason why

21

psychological traits *must* follow the pattern. Their distribution can only be established by measurement. But traits cannot be measured directly; they are inferred from behaviour. You cannot measure honesty, but only count up examples of honest behaviour. First a decision must be made as to what behaviour is going to be counted. And one of the arguments here is that it ought to be behaviour which will turn out to be normally distributed. Thus when new psychological tests are standardized, one criterion is their yielding the expected distribution. There is the clear danger of a circular argument, unless other evidence can be presented.

A fourth problem is that of the *origin* of individual differences, and particularly the relative contributions of nature and nurture, or heredity and environment (Chapter 12 and C1). And a fifth problem is that of *assessment and measurement*, with which we may group the question of appropriate methods of investigation (Chapters 5, 6).

3
Sir Francis Galton

Occasionally a leaflet drops through the letterbox demanding: 'Was an ape your grandfather?' and announcing a public meeting to refute the pernicious theory of evolution. So still reverberates the explosion touched off in 1859 by Charles Darwin's *Origin of Species*. The materials for the explosion had been accumulating for some time. They included a dawning scientific awareness of the existence of remains of unknown species of animals, and artefacts of primitive man; and a number of attempts to account for the multifarious variety of living things. Some of these (e.g. Erasmus Darwin, Charles's grandfather) supposed that the present complexity must somehow have *evolved* from an earlier simplicity. Darwin suggested, more simply and plausibly than others, how this might have come about.

Within every species, Darwin observed, there are widely ranging individual differences on a number of attributes which appear, moreover, to be inherited. By 'chance' (for the mechanisms of genetics were as yet unknown) some individuals are more aggressive, or swifter, or more subtly camouflaged, than others; in short, better equipped to survive longer and produce more offspring. These in turn will slowly, generation by generation, specialize more and more, each variety adapting to its environment which in turn is altered by its behaviour.

23

This view, which in its essentials is now almost universally held by biologists, had several vital consequences for psychological science. One was that animal behaviour was encouraged in its emergence as a subject of scientific study (see A3). Animals were related to men, but also man to animals. This view likewise fostered interest in the 'animal' nature of man, which appears clearly in Freud and has gone on ever since (e.g. Desmond Morris's *Naked Ape*). It helped to justify extrapolating from animals to men, a tendency for which psychologists have been strongly criticized, not always justly. Actually, of course, Darwin did not suppose that man is descended from apes. Both descend from far more remote common ancestors. Apes are our distant cousins, *homo sapiens* being the sole surviving representative of the family *hominidae*. Evolutionary theory stressed the adaptive value of variation; and this contributed to a favourable climate for the emergence of functionalist psychology, in which, in turn, the psychometric movement throve. Most important, the theory focused attention on individual variation among members of a species.

In particular it focused the attention of Francis Galton, another grandson of Erasmus Darwin. Galton is perhaps the least known of the three men who have most profoundly changed our view of human nature in modern times, the others being Darwin and Freud. Born in 1822, the youngest of seven, Francis Galton could read at two-and-a-half and sign his name when he was three. As a young man he studied both medicine and mathematics, without any great success. He found distasteful the primitive conditions of nineteenth-century hospitals – no antiseptics, no anaesthetics – and found too rigid the formal teaching of mathematics at Cambridge. He then for some years travelled extensively in the Near East and in Africa, still the Dark Continent. The travels resulted in books, and the books in Fellowship of the Royal Geographical Society. Travel likewise showed Galton the enormous variability between human groups. Reading Darwin's new theory in 1859 inspired him to attempt to solve this puzzle. Galton only devoted some twenty years of his long (he died in 1911) and intensely creative life to strictly psychological problems, and only some of these were concerned with individual differences. Nevertheless he was able to lay many of the foundations, still unchanged, of modern thinking.

Galton was an exceptionally inventive man (among his legacies to University College, London, was a collection of inventions, known as Galton's toys, for which he neglected to supply instructions. No one has succeeded in identifying the problems to which they were solutions). Among his attacks on the problem of individual differences was the method of composite photographs; images were superimposed so as to get a 'typical' Englishman or criminal (or the true face of Cleopatra, from coins, and remarkably ugly it was). Another line was fingerprinting, for the general adoption of which Galton was largely responsible. It was Galton who first suggested the study of twins to disentangle the effects of heredity and environment. For his first major psychological work, however, Galton took the family trees of eminent men – scholars, judges, athletes. His criterion of eminence was a statistical one: one in four thousand of the general population. He then found a strong tendency for an eminent individual in any one field to be related to others – there were, for example, forty-eight eminent sons for every hundred eminent fathers, far above the level of chance. Galton attributed this largely to heredity. Here he has been criticized for neglecting the effects of the privileged environment an eminent father might provide. Galton was, in fact, well aware of such effects, and the consensus of research since then undoubtedly gives a large role to heredity. Galton likewise compared whole cultures, on the basis of the achievements of its greatest men and the general level of education, thought and culture. Considering a normally distributed population (Fig. 2.1) as divided into sixteen equal grades, Galton concluded that his own Victorian society was two grades above the Negroes he had met on his travels, but two below the Greeks of the classical period.

Such conclusions led Galton to found the science of *eugenics*, which proposed to raise the general level of achievement by, for example, encouraging the more gifted to marry each other. Here, perhaps, his scientific optimism over-reached itself. It

25

was based, however, on one of the ways in which he was so original, namely trying to establish hard facts about human behaviour and human abilities, rather than relying upon reasoning, speculation, or anecdote. 'When', Galton asked in the *Fortnightly Review* in 1882, 'shall we have anthropometric laboratories, where a man may, when he pleases, get himself and his children weighed, measured and rightly photographed, and have their bodily faculties tested by the methods known to modern science?' Receiving no answer, he set up the laboratory himself. Visitors paid threepence for the record of their achievements, thus making Galton perhaps the only psychologist to be paid by his subjects rather than the other way round. At this laboratory in South Kensington was born the concept and practice of psychological testing.

We have given no more than a glimpse of Galton's seemingly limitless ingenuity (Karl Pearson's classic *Life* runs to three large volumes 1914; 1924; 1930). What Galton did (like, we would argue, Freud or Piaget) was to claim a new territory for scientific inquiry; to explore much of it himself, developing new theories and techniques on the way; and in so doing to give us a new view of ourselves. On this view, every ability and trait of man is amenable to measurement. The consequences of this view, for better or worse, are still working themselves out.

4
The scientific study of individual differences

The most immediate problem about the scientific study of individuals is whether it is possible at all. Gordon W. Allport (Chapter 17) has become famous for his advocacy of the view that unique human beings cannot be studied by science; for, he asserts, science deals with the general, not the unique. Several important (and persistent) issues are present in this controversy, and they need to be considered separately.

The general and the particular
First there is the assertion that science deals with the general. But this need not be so: Popper (1945) expresses the fallacy of Allport's argument when he distinguishes between the *historical sciences* and the *generalizing sciences*. The former include history, biography and *some* personality research; the latter include the natural sciences and related subjects. The ultimate aim of science, it is argued, is not to establish general or any other kind of laws, but to establish (or at least to approach) the truth – what is, was, and always will be the case. Peters (1958), following the Popperian argument, suggests that certain types of personality research are essentially biographies, and that they complement general principles.

Gordon Allport's position was a thorough and systematic one. He introduced into general psychological use the words *idiographic* and *nomothetic* (they were coined by Windelband, a nineteenth-century philosopher). According to Allport, prevailing personality research was nomothetic (dealing with groups) but should be idiographic (dealing with individuals). Allport produced several arguments to support this. First, he dismissed typologies; for, he says, they force the individual into a strait jacket, and lose his uniqueness. Moreover an individual might belong to several types, and these could interact uniquely in him, thus differentiating him from his neighbour who shares his membership of these types. The same applies to traits. Psychologists, Allport declares, have ignored the novelty that occurs when all a person's traits interact. Bannister and Fransella (1971) make the same point, when they express their disgust with the science of individual differences, saying that it is only the study of 'group sameness' (see F1).

Allport goes even further than this, however. He points out that apart from reducing individual differences to group sameness, valuable information is lost by supposing that all persons score somewhere on the same limited number of traits. He suggests that at the least we should recognize that there are strong 'personal dispositions' for each person, and that for each there are cardinal, central, and secondary traits. While this may be so, we may argue that there are basic fallacies in Allport's reasoning. The first is simply that he was engaged in a different enterprise from differential psychology. For differential psychology *is* the study of group sameness. Differential psychology, considered as one of the 'generalizing sciences', hopes to establish commonalities between persons (for example, traits) in order to allow comparisons to be made between individuals. Allport could be said to have confused differential psychology with another – equally valuable – enterprise, the art of biography. This, like history – of which in a sense it is a branch – is one of the descriptive sciences. Allport was in fact trying to put biography on a scientific basis (to this we might ascribe the title 'idiography').

A second error was to suppose that every person must be treated in a totally unique way, even apparently inventing a new language for each person. If there were an individual who was truly unique he would be incomprehensible, in fact not recognizable as an individual (which is why the most fantastic beings of science fiction have to have human traits). The attempt to give a unique description must produce chaos, as Holt (1962) has shown: for if a person is to be described *qua* person, terms of description which apply to others must be used, thus in principle assimilating the individual to the general (see D1).

In short, all description involves generalization. The scientific account of people, however, can concentrate either on the single case or on the general principles. The single case is usually tackled at a literary level, for example Boswell's life of Johnson. In all likelihood no other human being has ever existed, or will ever exist, with exactly Johnson's set of attributes – his scholarship, charity, prejudices, scrofula, compulsions, piety, devotion – and Boswell's record is apart from anything else an exceptional contribution to our understanding of human nature. It does not set out to be 'scientific'.

'Scientific' psychology

Much of psychology, on the other hand, does make such claims, either for individuals or, more usually, for groups. It is with the latter, therefore, that we are mainly concerned. It would, however, be misleading to suppose that we know what it is to be 'scientific'. For some decades now a group of philosophers, of whom the most famous is Karl Popper, have devoted themselves to this problem. One of their aims has been to find the distinguishing features of science. The enterprise has foundered. Toulmin (1970), reviewing the literature, declared that he could only say that 'science is what scientists do'. We will not enter that arena here, but wish to stress that the nature of scientific method is at the present time highly problematic.

We do follow the Popperians in supposing that science consists of the attempts to verify or falsify some proposition about reality. Note that this does not imply the need for experiments in the psychological sense; it only requires that one examine some part of the visible or sensible universe to see if one's idea or guess (theory and hypothesis are the grander names) is 'true', that is, consistent with the facts. A further step in

Popper's account is that the way to make progress is to state what would disprove the theory, and look to see if you can find it. If not, the theory continues to stand as the current best estimate of how things really are. This is more dubious, for various reasons (briefly discussed in D1).

Freud claimed that his theories were tested 'on the couch'; and this is often decried as not scientific, because not experimental. Not so: the weakness of the claim lies in the facts, first that the observations made in that situation are made by one person, which of course could easily be overcome; and secondly that the theories are often so imprecisely stated that almost *any* observation can be used as evidence for or against. The general principle of stating a hypothesis and checking it against reality is perfectly sound; and in this sense, as far as we can tell, any of the presumably infinite number of problems connected with individual differences can be treated scientifically; but in practice, only a few have received attention, and only a few useful strategies have emerged.

Control and analysis

Two respects in which psychology offers something new, however, not offered by philosophy, history, or literature, are the attempt to *control variables*, and the application of *numerical analysis* (see A8). Indeed these are done only in a much less sophisticated way even by the other social sciences. Many of the problems of individual differences do not lend themselves to controlling variables: you can hardly rear children with what are believed to be impoverished environments, or deliberately manipulate their genetic endowment. The second set of techniques therefore come to the fore. E. L. Thorndike (1874–1949), the inventor of the Law of Effect, one of the foundations of psychological learning theory (see A3), proclaimed, 'Whatever exists, exists in some quantity and can, in principle, be measured.' With this Galton would doubtless have agreed: and it is from him, and in particular from his concept of correlation, that we start. Correlation, the extent to which two measures co-vary, is expressed as a coefficient between $+1$ (exact agreement and -1 (an exact inverse relationship). 0 indicates no relationship. The coefficient can be calculated by several methods, the most precise being that devised by Galton's pupil Karl Pearson, and yielding a statistic known as Pearson's 'r'. Other comparable statistics are Spearman's rs or rho and Kendall's tau (see A8).

Factor analysis

Correlation, important in its own right, is also the foundation of *factor analysis*, developed by Pearson's students and colleagues, Charles Spearman and Cyril Burt, and by the American, L. L. Thurstone. Factor analysis is essentially a test of multiple correlation. In the simpler case, which is sometimes known as a 'bivariate' test, there are only two variables. Factor analysis is *multivariate*. There is no theoretical upper limit to the number of variables, but in practice it is rare to use more than a hundred. The calculations, even with the use of computers as is normal, become colossal, and the justification of choice of variables becomes difficult. The object of factor analysis is not to find a correlation coefficient for every pair of variables; but to determine the smallest number of categories of co-variates into which the data fall.

Suppose, to give a favourite example, we wanted to investigate athletic ability. A natural starting point would be the accepted events of an athletics meeting. We could get, say, the members of several athletics clubs to compete in all the events, and factor analyse, that is correlate, all their performances. Almost certainly some individuals would do well at distance races, others at sprints and long jump, others still at throwing events. Performances within each group of events would probably correlate quite highly, whereas correlations between each group would be much lower. Thus we might be led to conclude that we had isolated three main constituents of athletic ability or *factors*. Each event would have a relationship with each factor, called its *loading* on that factor. We might go further and name the factors: say, stamina, speed, and power. We might go on to talk of performers having a lot of stamina (as indeed we do). And since the existence of stamina had been scientifically demonstrated by careful measurements and statistical analysis, as well as according with common sense, it might easily seem that we now had good explanations.

This is a fairly close analogy of what is done for psychological characteristics. Measurements are taken of behaviour that seems to be appropriate. It may be real-life situations, but more often tasks are invented specially, in order to keep them the same for all subjects. From the correlations between these, factors emerge. Now the athletics example shows several of the problems with this. First of all how do we know what to measure? Athletic events are largely arbitrary, or at any rate the result of tradition. Classical Greek athletics, for example, had only two foot races, roughly corresponding to our 200 and 1500 metres. The Watusi tribe in Africa are keen on high jumping, but take off from a little mound. What about weight-lifting? And so on. In principle there is no end to the selection. What of different conditions (e.g. the Olympics in high-altitude Mexico City)? The only, incomplete safeguard is to be aware of this – and to continue to seek further evidence. How much greater a problem this is with psychological measurement can readily be seen when (for example) in a different culture the very task itself may be meaningless (see C5).

The next danger is that having isolated a group of correlations, we assume we know what it means because we know what we put into it. But that, of course, is part of what we are trying to find out. And the next danger is that it may be assumed that the factor is an entity, rather than simply an abstraction. Why did X win the race? Because he had more stamina. But stamina is not a commodity you can buy: it is a description of a condition, based on observations. We only say that X has stamina because he holds out longer than others. Similarly we only say that Y is intelligent, or honest, because he consistently gets problems right or pays his fare on the bus. It is misleading to think that intelligence or honesty is a kind of force inside Y causing him to act like this. (This should not be confused with the fact that Y may *value* honesty as an ideal, and strive for it.)

It might be argued that surely we all know roughly what it means to be honest, or intelligent, and it is simply a matter of discovering to what extent traits tend to go together, and how

32

much of them each person has. Indeed Burt (1968), one of the foremost exponents of the technique, has criticized other investigators, during the period when behaviourism was dominant, for not checking their results against common sense and introspective evidence. It is also true, as Butcher (1968) argues, that factor analysis (and related techniques such as cluster analysis) constitute the most powerful means we have for showing what is common and what is specific in a complex sample of behaviour. Certainly, by this means a convincing picture has been obtained of many human traits and abilities, the basis of very extensive practical applications in therapy, education, selection, and so forth.

The reflexive nature of psychology

The basic difficulty is a more profound one, which underlies all the problems we have discussed. It resides in the reflexive nature of psychology: psychologists try to investigate objectively a subject-matter of which they themselves are part. Further, every human characteristic only counts as such because it appears to be important in a particular sample of the human race. The total human population is to all intents and purposes infinite: for who can say with precision when men ceased to be animals, or what they might become in the future? (Two further themes explored, more than trivially, by science fiction.) Records of much are, besides, irrecoverably lost. Still further, psychological knowledge must in turn affect behaviour, as it demonstrably does. This provides one argument why psychology can never emulate physics: the reality psychologists hope to approximate must by definition be a shifting one.

5
The basis of psychological assessment

There can be no doubt that the attempt to apply quantitative methods to human beings has been one of the most powerful influences in shaping our society. Take one example, the so-called 'eleven-plus' (it was really ten-plus). As is well known, the 1944 Education Act envisaged three sorts of secondary education for Great Britain: grammar, technical, and 'modern'. For some years virtually all children were assessed at the age of ten and assigned to one of the three, a system which in 1975 has not yet quite given place to 'comprehensive' schooling. The arguments about this are based upon politics and emotion, and not, whatever the protagonists claim, upon evidence. But there can be no doubt that the system, whatever its merits or demerits, could hardly have arisen without the assumptions of psychology. In particular, the assumption that an individual's abilities and dispositions can be accurately assessed in an hour or so, enabling predictions to be made for at least the next five years ahead. It is not just that psychologists supplied the tools: they invented the concept, a quite new one in human history.

Of course examinations are not new, and in China officers of state had been thus selected for many centuries. In the nineteenth century, Britain introduced competitive entry to the public service. No doubt the latter, and the testing movement, both reflected general cultural trends. But psychological tests mark an important innovation, in several respects. First there was the attempt to assimilate human beings, and human performance, to other natural phenomena, and the conclusion that they were distributed in the same kind of way, i.e. 'normally'. Second there was the belief that one could isolate some kind of basic psychological dimensions to measure, almost independent of actual achievement. Third there was the implication, that seemed to follow, that human abilities were relatively fixed and unalterable; which was supported likewise by the emphasis on hereditary factors.

Assessment

Now 'assessment' covers several activities. One may, for example, try to assess oneself, that is to say try to gain insight, self-understanding, or the like. And we all constantly assess other people, make judgments about them, what they think and feel and are likely to do. Psychological assessment may include similar activities although, psychologists hope, on a more systematic basis; and it also includes tests and measurements. In the attempt to assess people, a distinction is often made between *understanding* and *explaining*; and some writers such as the German psychologist, Spranger (1928), suppose that we have a special faculty of intuitive understanding (*verstehen*). By this we are able to know directly what another person is like – not always with the same degree of accuracy, of course. Such a view has not been popular with British or American psychologists, because it seems to defy Thorndike's principle of measurement. Undoubtedly we do often have the experience of seeming to know another person very directly; but to the present authors it seems preferable to consider this in terms of a close and flexible 'internal model' (see D1).

It is explaining that is more often said to be the aim of science, and this is often linked with the hope of predicting and/or controlling the phenomena, on the one hand; and with measurement, on the other. None of these links is absolutely necessary; we can certainly predict without explaining and without measuring. On the whole, however, the aim of psychological assessment has been to devise quantitative measures based on theoretical and testable explanations. Many attempts, of course, have fallen far short of this aim.

This is partly because, as we have hinted, psychometrics and testing came to be almost a separate branch of psychology, often cut off from the experimental side and even, to some extent, from psychotherapy, just as the latter two have frequently had little contact with each other. To many people, psychologists were testers. It was an activity which quite quickly became respectable, no doubt partly because of its useful practical applications. It is interesting to note, however, the four main meanings the OED lists for tests: a critical examination or trial; a standard against which something is judged; a ground for admission or rejection; a chemical test, e.g. for the presence of some substance.

Tests

We must say something more about the basis of tests, as the psychological assessment *par excellence* (see E2). Part of the doctrine of tests is that they should be valid and reliable. *Reliability* is really consistency. Obviously a ruler would be no good if it varied in length, and for this reason standards of length are so constructed as to be unaffected by changes in temperature or other conditions. A psychological test, ideally, should give the same result every time it is applied to an identical subject, or the same subject under identical conditions. We do not know that either of these situations ever exists. Indeed the best evidence for them would be test results, so that the problem becomes circular. Reliability is generally supported in two ways. Tests can be given twice to the same subjects, sufficiently long apart that responses are unlikely to be remembered, yet not so long that the subjects will have greatly altered (the test-retest method). It is never possible to be certain that these criteria are met. In the split-half method, items in a test are randomly divided into two groups. In either case, agreement between the two sets of results is taken to be evidence of reliability. It is not conclusive, but it is the best we have.

Validity refers to the question of whether we know what we are measuring. This is a far trickier problem still, since we do

36

not know what we ought to be measuring. The general answer to the problem is to compare the results with some other criterion. Binet compared his original test results with the judgments of teachers. Several varieties of validity assessment can be distinguished. Cronbach (1960) gives four. *Predictive validity* means checking the results of the test against future performance of the subjects, such as success in school, recovery from illness, appearances in court, or whatever the test is supposed to be related to. Usually the relationship is that the test is meant to give an estimate of some quality, such as intelligence, which contributes significantly to the behaviour we are interested in. It would be quite possible to have tests which were actual samples of that behaviour (rather like taking one 'trial' driving lesson). Such tests could have very high predictive validity, but would be useful only in one situation. *Concurrent validation* merely means that the two measures (test and performance) are taken at the same or nearly the same time. *Content validation* means looking to see if the test items are relevant to what is being examined. This only applies to simple cases – items in a history test should be on the syllabus. A version of this is face validity: does the test look plausible? There is no theoretical reason why it should, yet total implausibility may be a warning sign. *Construct validation* is more sophisticated. A measure should be derived from some theory, which will have other testable consequences. In this respect a psychological test is like an experiment. Few attempt this, and fewer still succeed.

Theory

The reason, of course, (apart from laziness or ignorance of scientific method) is a shortage of good psychological theories. The choice of what to measure may be derived from three main sorts of source: from guesswork or intuition; from a general, more-or-less organized set of assumptions; or from something more resembling a full scientific theory. Thus many early tests of 'intelligence' were based on the individual psychologist's conviction that intelligence 'really is' the ability to solve problems, or to benefit from experience, or what not. The F Test became famous as a measure of 'authoritarianism'. It was derived by its inventors, Adorno and others (1949) from psychoanalytic assumptions about personality development, but has subsequently turned out to be highly inconsistent and not very predictive. Attempts to set the study of individual differences upon more sound theoretical bases have been made by, among others, Burt, Eysenck, Cattell, Guilford, and Vernon.

However, partly due to the lack of generally agreed theory, proponents of measurements are at variance on a large number of issues. We have already mentioned the idiographic *v.* nomothetic problem. Then are we to concentrate on assessing separate aspects of the individual, perhaps with the ultimate aim of reconstructing him from the parts; or are we to make some attempt to deal with him as a whole from the start? Another issue concerns structure and function. There seems no reason in principle why a psychological theory cannot accommodate both, but in practice American theories, at least since William James (1842–1910), have tended to concentrate on function, emphasizing the pragmatic, business-like side of behaviour. The classical German psychology of Wundt (1832–1920) was concerned with structure and recently the structuralism of Piaget and Lévi-Strauss has brought this perhaps more static, more philosophical orientation to the fore again.

On the other hand a static approach can be contrasted with a dynamic one. In this respect the attempt of Freud to deal with a form of psychic energy and its vicissitudes stands against the more mechanical model of behaviourism (see C1, D3). Again, an explanation can be offered in terms of the past, the present, or the future. Freud believed that much (though not all) behaviour was the result of events early in childhood. Kurt Lewin (1890–1947) concentrated on the forces acting on the individual in the present. William McDougall (1871–1938) felt that the goals towards which behaviour is directed offer a better and more general clue. Are we to treat our individual as subject or object? Are we to concentrate on what we can see happens to him, or on his experience of what is happening?

Choice of theory

And so on. Brian Little (1972) goes so far as to suggest that personality theories derive from the personality of the theorist, which he tries to make the general model. (It has been said that the real title of every book ever written is, *How to be more like me*, and this is as true of psychology texts as any others.) Even with the use of factor analysis (and still more so without it) there is a degree of arbitrariness in both what the investigator thinks worth investigating and what he does with his results. Thus, for example, the most massive of all theories of intellectual development, that of Piaget, has concentrated on how knowledge is acquired (epistemology) and on the complex structures thought to underlie this. It has not directly yielded a reliable and valid instrument for measuring development, as might have been expected. Or compare the analyses of intellectual functioning offered respectively by Burt and Guilford. In Burt's system, there is one general factor – 'innate general cognitive ability' or 'g' – which underlies all tasks involving 'intelligence'; then there are group factors such as verbal, spatial, or numerical ability; then there are factors specific to particular tasks. It is a hierarchical system. Guilford, on the other hand, postulates 120 separate factors of which a particular selection are involved in any task. Both, of course, present massive evidence in support, but it is hard to avoid concluding that the systems at least partly originate from the theorists' personal preferences. It has even been suggested that Burt's account resembles a British constitutional monarchy, and Guilford's a federation of United States. (The analogy is originally Spearman's.)

It is for such reasons that construct validity is sought. Consider the case of Eysenck's personality theory. The dimension of introversion-extraversion is supported by factor analytic studies, but Eysenck has sought to check his theory in many other ways. Those with high scores either way, for example, should behave differently in social situations – *other* than those put into the factor analysis. It is comparatively easy to see if this is so, and thus establish predictive (or concurrent) validity.

However, Eysenck can claim to have established construct

validity also. The argument, reduced to its simplest, is that there are innate differences in human (and other) nervous systems, presumably normally distributed, such that individuals respond differently to conditioning (see A3). Since the theory holds, following Pavlov and the learning theorists, that conditioning is basic to learning, it will be the case that some individuals learn social rules, for example, better than others. These are introverted, and the extreme case would be socially inhibited and in a constant state of nervous anxiety. Extraverts, on the other hand, learn less well: the extreme is a psychopath who has hardly learned any of the rules of normal social behaviour. Thus the theory predicts quite clearly that introverts, as assessed by psychological tests, should condition more readily than extraverts. This is amenable to experiment and Eysenck reports that it is, indeed, the case. Similarly introverts should be less susceptible to alcohol, but more so to punishment, and so on. Of course there is far more to the theory than this, and this is not the place to assess the vast amount of experimental evidence now available, some of it contradictory (see D3). The point to be made is that this is the outstanding example of an attempt to develop an account of individual differences according to the normal principles of scientific investigation.

6
The practice of assessment

The psychometrics industry is a bit like the motor car industry. It has its standard models that go on seemingly for ever, and it has its nine-day wonders; it has economy products and luxury products. Some countries favour official or semi-official tests, others prefer private enterprise. Any producer, to survive, must sell; and any test must offer something to the user. Good ones must offer some kind of reliability, though it is remarkable how long certain products can survive on claims that are highly dubious. One reason for this is that in many human situations it can be better to do almost anything rather than nothing. Another reason is that in practical situations it is often extremely difficult to carry out controlled studies. Men may be selected to be salesmen, or school-leavers to be university students, and most of them do fairly well at it. But it is very hard to get good evidence that they would not have done even better at something else, or that other individuals would not have done as well as those selected. The very fact of having been selected – or rejected – may itself influence what an individual does.

Standardization
In order to get some degree of respectability, a test or other psychological measurement must be *standardized*. Once again

the concept stems from Galton, who was perhaps the first to see that individual performance can only be compared against that of other individuals. Of course the making of comparative judgments was not new: what was new was the establishment of the distribution of performance from a defined population, thus giving a dimension upon which any individual can be placed. We now talk of this in terms of different scales of measurement, and commonly distinguish four (see A8).

Scales of measurement

In a *nominal* scale all we do is categorize. An army squad numbering is using a nominal scale; classifying people as right- or left-handed is the same thing. An *ordinal* scale puts the items in rank order: the army drill manoeuvre of sizing is doing this – the men end up tallest on the right, shortest on the left, but the difference between any adjacent pair may be large or small. Grades in school may do this: we know who is top, but not by how much. That additional information is contained in an *interval* scale, as it would be if marks were supplied or heights measured. An interval scale is such that the distance between any two adjacent points on it is equal to that between any other two. The scales on thermometers are of this type, and psychologists try to make their scales like this, so that measuring intelligence or extraversion would be at least as sophisticated as taking a temperature. However they by no means always succeed. In a *ratio* scale it is possible to start from an absolute zero. A few, but not many, psychological measures are of this kind (e.g. reaction times).

The advance in the development of psychological dimensions consists in moving from a nominal scale (men as either phlegmatic or choleric or . . .) to an ordinal scale (men arranged in order of brightness, honesty, achievement . . .) to an interval scale (we can tell by how much one exceeds another).

To achieve this, standardizing involves, among other processes, some of them too technical to discuss here, devising a set of items (questions) and trying them out on a large and supposedly 'standard' population. Some items turn out to be more valid and reliable than others and are retained; others are rejected or modified. Finally we end up with norms for the completed test, that is to say the distribution of scores made by our standard or comparison population. It is this process (greatly oversimplified here) that is intended to justify the inclusion of any particular item, which taken alone may seem unlikely or implausible. Against the norms obtained any new test result is compared. This brings out again the *relative* nature of psychological measurement. It is obvious that a test cannot be standardized on the whole population of even a small country, let alone the world and still less the whole human population that has ever lived or will ever live. Our standard population is only a small selection, which we try to make representative. But the choice of criteria by which we decide this is itself a psychological decision. To standardize a new test of intelligence we need some intelligent people. But how do we know they are intelligent?

Types of assessment

Nevertheless on this basis a multitude of tests has appeared, some well standardized, some not at all. 'Tests' in fact, while a frequently used shorthand, should be restricted to only some forms of assessment, perhaps most strictly, to cases where there are right and wrong answers. Methods of assessment can be grouped or classified in many ways, for example by the phenomena they are meant to measure, by the sorts of response required, the conditions of administration (such as to groups or individually), etc. One common grouping, suggested by Rosenzweig (1948), is into:

(a) subjective: those where the main emphasis is on an observation or report made by the subject on himself;
(b) objective: those where the observation is made by someone else;
(c) projective: those where some aspect of the individual is 'projected' into some stimulus or situation.

There are still other methods – such as interviews and some group techniques – that do not fit readily into this classification,

43

and Allport (1937) proposed a list of eleven types which he thought the smallest useful number. These were as follows:

1. *Constitutional and physiological diagnosis.* This includes measurement of body build, heart rate, electrical activity of the brain (EEG), action of the glands, etc.
2. *Sociocultural studies.* The facts of age, sex, occupation, class, race, roles, etc.
3. *Personal documents and case studies.* Useful data can include autobiographies, letters, diaries, pen portraits. While subject to many provisos – obviously such documents are completely un-standardized and open to multiple interpretation – such materials often enable us to approach the individual's private world of experience.
4. *Self-appraisal.* There are many ways of making this more systematic, including techniques such as the WAY – asking 'Who are you?'; and Q-sorts, where the subject sorts a series of statements according to whether he thinks they apply to himself.
5. *Conduct sampling.* Observations of behaviour can be made more manageable by, for example, time sampling, where what is recorded is what action a subject is performing say every five minutes. Sometimes subjects are put in 'miniature situations' designed to elicit revealing behaviour. Allport includes interviews in this category.
6. *Ratings.* Here an observer, usually one who knows the subject well, assesses him on a number of scales, often against a known population (say, other students taught by the rater).
7. *Tests and scales.* In this group come the more closely defined psychological measuring instruments, which may seek to assess intelligence or other intellectual qualities, personality traits and dispositions, abilities, aptitudes and interests, etc. The list of published tests and scales runs into many hundreds, and this is not the place to attempt individual assessments.
8. *Depth analysis.* Techniques developed for therapy, such as free association, can of course also be used for assessment.
9. *Expressive behaviour.* This includes for example gestures, posture, handwriting, from which some information can be

gained (though less than might be claimed by professional graphologists).

10. *Projective techniques.* The notion derives from Freud, and is essentially that submerged aspects of personality will be 'projected' into neutral or ambiguous stimuli, of which the Rorschach ink-blots are probably the most famous. (Rorschach testing has an extensive literature and lengthy training courses, but its worth remains questionable.) Probably such techniques are of greatest use in helping to fill out a picture of an individual by suggesting points that might otherwise be overlooked.

11. *Synoptic procedures.* Allport uses this term for methods of combining information from different sources to gain a picture of the total person.

All of these categories contain many variations, and all have advantages and disadvantages. Do they work? As so often, it depends on what you mean, or on what you want.

Uses of assessment

Assessment is probably most commonly and usefully employed for some kind of prediction. We want to know whether someone will make a good engineer or salesman, or benefit from some treatment or special education, and so on. Despite the difficulties previously mentioned, the balance of evidence is absolutely clear, and has been for many years, that prediction using well-established psychological methods is superior to any other approach, from lay intuition to astrology. On the whole, standardized techniques are the most readily applicable to any situation, but useful information can be got by other means. Methods, such as interviewing, or ratings by other people, which are not strictly psychological in themselves – inasmuch as everyone does them to a certain extent anyway – can be vastly improved by even simple training. For example interviewers can be taught how to create a relaxed and sympathetic atmosphere, how to distinguish the important from the trivial, how to order and use the information they gain. The object is not to trick the person interviewed, but to gain a more realistic picture of him (see E2).

Another main use of assessment methods is as an aid in guidance, usually involving some increase in self-understanding. Here the situation is at once more complex. We are giving an individual information about himself which is necessarily both incomplete and relative. Probably the safest guide is to emphasize the positive side, and try to show the client a wider range of opportunities than he had appreciated (see F3).

A third important use is in research. Some of the theoretical puzzles have been touched on. And they bring us back to the distinction between understanding and explaining. To assess a person may mean to make some judgment about him, a sort of examination. As we have suggested, there are many ways of improving such judgments. It may mean trying to comprehend the person, to understand him in an intuitive or empathic way. Psychological techniques can probably improve this ability, though it is hard to prove it conclusively. It may imply some sort of explanation of behaviour, and this in turn may imply seeking basic or fundamental dimensions, with all the problems attending them.

Dangers and difficulties

There are other problems. Like many other disciplines concerned with people, psychometrics is not free from those best described as charlatans. Some peddle spurious 'tests' to gullible businessmen; others offer to the general public fake personality assessments whose ultimate purpose is to entangle the individual in 'courses' or 'treatment' of value only to the vendors. In some countries such activities are illegal, partly because it is, of course, those individuals most in need of genuine help who are vulnerable. With our more lenient laws, the best recourse at present is to seek advice through the appropriate professional body, the British Psychological Society.

One thing on which professionals would agree is that single assessments, and test results in particular, are meaningless, and even dangerous, without interpretation. Just as a high temperature may help to indicate, to a physician, one of many disorders (or none); so a particular test score is just one piece of information whose interpretation requires skill and experience.

Then there is the no-man's-land of moral judgment. A great deal of fuss is made over whether one racial or cultural group scores higher or lower than another on tests of intelligence. This is first of all a question of fact; either they do or they don't. Second of all, such results *may* tell us something about the nature of intellectual abilities, or about capacity to undertake certain other tasks. The matter becomes controversial when value is attached to the facts, so that one particular pattern of scores is seen as somehow better than another. This is very easily done, since high scores on intelligence tests are correlated with success in what has latterly been the dominant culture – naturally, since that is where they were created and standardized. Many would argue (and we agree) that the value of psychological traits is relative to the culture in which they develop, just as tall, thin physiques are better adapted to hot climates, and short, thickset ones to cold.

The most obvious danger of testing is that it has effects on those tested. Unless the results are confined to a solitary scientist, some consequences are likely to follow for the individual. He may be treated differently by others; he may regard himself differently. So-called 'radical' psychologists (see Brown, 1973) claim that testing is positively harmful. The view almost seems to be, not just that individuals may be disadvantaged by their classification, but that it is wrong to classify people at all, for fear that we thereby reduce them to objects (see F8). On the other hand Hudson (1966) claimed that psychometrics had made little or no progress in the previous forty years: it was not so much harmful as trivial. Perhaps both these criticisms stem from the fact that, so far, no one has shown convincingly how to justify any classification theoretically.

7
R. B. Cattell

A recent interview with Professor R. B. Cattell begins with these illuminating words:

> Raymond Cattell fervently believes that personality theory will one day take its place among the sciences. His vision is not the least humble. He fully expects that man will be able to predict an individual's behaviour with the kind of accuracy with which he now predicts the movements of the planets. Cattell is a mathematician. An individual's personality, he believes, submits to mathematical formulation in the same way our solar system submits to Kepler's laws of planetary motion. (*Psychology Today*, July 1973.)

Cattell is almost aggressively determined that his aim should be reached, and he is not afraid to denounce those who scorn precise measurement. He believes that factor analysis (see p.31) is the key to these problems, and that it is one of the best tools ever invented by man. He was instrumental in founding the Society for Multivariate Experimental Psychology in 1960, and served as its first president. In his recent book *Beyondism* (1974), he tries to show how the human race can be improved by scientifically studying people and their interrelations.

Cattell's written style is scholarly and sometimes imperious.

As a person, however, he is 'engaging, reticent, a good listener, concerned to discount those qualities of fearsomeness which have been attributed to him'. (ibid)

Raymond B. Cattell was born in England in 1905 and grew up in Staffordshire, where he spent much time out of doors, sailing. He claims to have traced his lineage back to a common ancestor with James McKeen Cattell, the early American mental tester. Like Eysenck, he studied at the University of London, where he met Burt and Spearman, who supervised his PhD. His first degree was in chemistry and physics at the early age of nineteen. After turning to psychology Cattell became a lecturer at University College, Exeter, and later, from 1932 to 1937, was Director of the City Psychological Clinic, Leicester, thus (like Burt and Eysenck) gaining extensive practical as well as academic experience. In 1937 Cattell moved to America, and has remained there since. He was initially a research associate with E. L. Thorndike (of 'Law of Effect' fame) at Teachers College, Columbia. In 1945 he went to the University of Illinois at Champaign, where he remains. His second wife, whom he married in 1946, is a mathematician working in the same field as her husband, and a publisher of personality tests. Cattell has five children of whom two are mathematical psychologists, thus (as with Eysenck) lending support to their father's heredity theories.

Also like Eysenck (and Burt and Piaget, for that matter) Cattell has been remarkably prolific. He has published thirty books and monographs and over three hundred research articles. He says that it is unlikely that he possesses more energy than most people, but that he manages his time better. Oddly enough, Cattell has not taken his own personality test, but he says that he matches up to the typical research worker's profile: introverted, high ego strength, high IQ.

Cattell has worked in a very large number of fields: intelligence and its measurement; personality and its assessment; psychopathology, motivation, cross-cultural studies, morality, etc. In *Beyondism* he proposes 'a new morality for science', and suggests five basic changes to society (the book is in some ways a challenge to Skinner's *Beyond Freedom and Dignity*):

49

1 A democratic basis for evaluating wants, but technocratic machinery to satisfy those wants administered by specialists.
2 A ministry of evolution 'directing change from the top instead of the bottom of society'.
3 Abolition of archaic political stereotypes: left, right, liberal, fascist, and so on.
4 Psychological selection and social science teaching for politicians.
5 Acceptance of evolutionary ethical values in place of dogmatic religious ones in social legislation.

Beyondism, like Galton's *Hereditary Genius*, makes an argument for eugenic experimentation. One of the main problems with this would seem to be that of deciding what are the qualities whose value is so unquestionable that they can safely be developed at the cost of others.

The basic work of Cattell, however, has been the use of factor analysis in the elucidation of the basic dimensions of personality. Using personality questionnaires, subjective tests, objective tests of various kinds, and other measures, Cattell and his colleagues claim to have identified the sixteen to twenty most important factors. Cattell's account of personality is in terms of *traits*. It might thus seem contradictory to Eysenck's *type* theory, but this is not so, since Eysenck has explained types as the outcome of two major dimensions. Each of these would subsume a number of Cattell's dimensions. It is the level of analysis that differentiates the two approaches. Cattell's main published personality measuring instrument, the 16 PF (personality factor) takes the form of a questionnaire yielding a profile of the individual, with a score on each of the sixteen traits (see D3). As already explained, there is no reason why traits identified through factor analysis should correspond to those of everyday language; and Cattell's mostly have rather technical names such as parmia, premsia, or coasthenia, though some such as excitability or shrewdness are more familiar.

Cattell and his colleagues have carried out extremely extensive standardizing procedures, and their measuring instruments can claim quite high degrees of both reliability and validity. They have been able successfully to predict behaviour in diverse situations from knowing a person's scores. Indeed Cattell summarizes his general viewpoint in the formula:

$$R = f(S.P.)$$

This means that *behaviour* (Response) is a function of the *stimulus situation* and the nature of the individual's *personality*. This brings out three points. Cattell is an avowed behaviourist; he is less interested in experience since that is not amenable (he argues) to measurement, without which science cannot advance. Secondly Cattell uses 'personality' to mean 'that which tells what a man will do when placed in a given situation', which virtually embraces all possible psychological facts. Thirdly it raises the problem of what is a situation, one which Cattell has tried to answer by devising a taxonomy or classification of situations. Cattell is perfectly well aware that personality does not remain constant from moment to moment but is affected by mood and role, to name only two variables.

Cattell exemplifies very well what we might term 'optimistic science'. By patient measurement and sophisticated analysis, we shall come at last to understand human personality in all its complexity, and so be able to adjust behaviour to that which we prefer.

8
Personality and individuality

A number of further puzzles arise from the study of personality and individuality. They are due partly to the variety of meanings words may have. 'Personality', for example, in the OED means: 'Being a person; personal existence or identity; distinctive personal character; person'. As often happens, psychologists have taken up a word in general use, and employed it for technical reasons. However they have not agreed on what these are. Thus 'personality' may be used as an integrating concept by some (Freud, for example) while for others, such as Kelly, it serves rather to differentiate individuals (see D3). Puzzlement also arises from an ambivalence on the part of psychologists towards personality and its assessment. There is the conflict between the desire to study individuals for themselves, as individuals, unique persons, and the wish to examine what they share. Occasionally, as in the case of G. W. Allport, the conflict becomes explicit.

Norms
It may seem rather obvious that psychologists working in this area have as their subject-matter individual human beings. However this is not the only possibility open to psychologists. They might prefer for example – and often have done – to concentrate on whatever fundamental processes may perhaps

underlie the variegated behaviour of individuals. E. G. Boring, the historian of experimental psychology, saw this as one of the watersheds between the classical German approach of Wundt and his followers, and the emerging American schools. Given that it is individuals in which we are interested, there is a choice between taking them singly or in groups; between their unique and their shared characteristics. As Kluckhohn and Murray (1953) put it, every man is in some respects (a) like all other men (universal norms); (b) like some other men (group norms); (c) like no other men (idiosyncratic norms). Psychology should of course be interested in all of these. In practice by far the greatest attention has been paid to (b). Universal norms are, strictly speaking, impossible to establish by investigation since we cannot, of course, study all human beings. Those of which we can be certain – e.g. all human beings must be alive, must have a reasonable complement of bodily organs – are usually of little psychological interest. The attempt to establish idiosyncratic norms meets difficulties we have already discussed. Most psychologists have elected to study groups, that is some *sample* of people. However these distinctions have often been far from clear, and investigators have given the impression, or perhaps believed, that in establishing norms for some group they are actually discovering something universal. Allport, perhaps the only major psychologist to concentrate on idiosyncratic norms, was likewise in fact working on area (b).

Idiography

We suggested in Chapter 3 that a science of individual persons was possible, and that it might be called idiography. Rosenzweig (1958) proposed that the study of individual *norms* be called *idiodynamics*. Idiography would refer rather to the gathering of information about an individual from whatever source might be available: historical material, contemporary observations, or, best of all, experiment. It would thus be much wider than what is normally covered by what is called 'the case-study method' which depends, in the main, on biographical details, test scores, and interview data. Something rather like this was presented by Smith, Bruner, and White (1956) in a book called *Opinions and Personality*. This was a study in depth of a small number of individuals in an attempt to understand and in at least some sense explain their behaviour and attitudes. The approach does not seem to have been followed up. There might even be a useful interaction between the art of biography and the science of idiography. The fact that large numbers of intensive studies of individuals appear every year with, it is not unfair to say, little more than a colour-supplement knowledge of Freud by way of psychological expertise reflects strangely on one or both disciplines. There might of course be a slight problem in that the eminent subjects of biography have strong tendencies to be busy, uninterested, or dead, and so unavailable for experimentation.

The self

Some other problems in which 'personality' and 'individuality' intertwine centre round the concept of the *self* (see F7). There is the question as to how it comes about that there is a more-or-less continuous sensation of individuality or personal identity in each of us – what William James called 'the verifiable ground of personal identity'. Presumably this must largely arise from the fact that each individual has unique physical characteristics and unique experiences. It is a matter for philosophy, or science fiction, whether if there were two identical individuals they would feel themselves to be two or one. It seems likely, however, that the sensation of individuality varies in strength from one person to another. And it would appear to vary in popularity: some aim in general to be as like other members of their group as possible, while a few deliberately try to be different (though it is common experience that rejection of one set of standards is often little more than adoption of those of another group).

Maturity

This is closely linked with another question, namely the way in which an individual integrates his psychological components, and thus achieves a patterned individuality, a mature personality. It is plausible to suppose that the greater the extent to which this happens, the greater will be the variability between individuals. This should not be confused with two popular concepts: one, that of being 'a personality' in the sense of a celebrity. Television chat shows have made us familiar with many famous persons who emerge as quite unremarkable for anything save the specialized talent that brought them success (and sometimes not even that). The other concept is that of 'a strong personality', that is to say dominant and forceful. These are traits which individuals can possess in high degree (and which can be measured, for example by the 16 P.F.) without necessarily being high on others. The *distinctness* of different traits is precisely what it has been possible to show scientifically for the first time by the use of factor analysis. It is a mistake to think that the person who generally gets his own way is necessarily the wisest or most intelligent, and examples abound throughout history and in everyday experience of the unfortunate consequences of trusting to the judgment of leaders.

The self-concept

From the psychologist's point of view the issues that present themselves are those of measuring and of explaining. Some, but not much, progress has been made with each. As far as assessment is concerned, the tendency is to concentrate on the *self-concept*: a person's notion or idea of himself. Some information about this can be got from most of the methods listed in Chapter 6. With a view to greater objectivity, however, two or three approaches have been particularly developed. In the Q-sort technique, it will be recalled, a subject is asked to classify a series of statements, trait names, or other kinds of items according to how well he thinks they apply to himself. He can also sort them according to his idea of how he would *like* to be, or how he thinks he appears to others. The results can be correlated to discover, for example, how closely and in what ways the subject feels he matches up to his own ideal. Cattell, as part of his attempt to assess personality comprehensively, has analysed what he terms the *self-sentiment*. This is assessed by a set of items such as 'I like to have good control over all my mental processes – my memory, impulses and general behavior', or 'I want to be first-rate in my job'. The subject is asked to agree or disagree. It should be stressed that such items are not just invented *ad hoc*: they are items that have been shown to be loaded on the self-sentiment factor.

A rather different approach comes from the work of George Kelly (see D3, F1). Kelly took a particular view about human nature, which may be simplified by saying that he regarded man as a scientist – we are constantly engaged, as it were, in forming hypotheses about the nature of the world, and testing these against reality as best we may. It thus becomes important, if we are to understand an individual's behaviour, to get an idea of how he perceives the world, or, as Kelly expressed it, of the nature of his *constructs*. The range of constructs a person may have is wide, and subject to change. But it is not so great or so labile that it cannot be assessed. For this purpose Kelly devised what is known as *repertory grid* technique (see F1). It has a number of variations, but depends essentially on getting the subject to classify events, experiences, persons, or other items in ways that seem important to him. One way to do this is to make a list of persons with whom the subject interacts. Then his task is to take these in groups of three and in each case say why two of them are alike and different from the third. For example mother and sister might be alike in being seen as affectionate; father is different, being seen as rejecting. The various responses are entered on a chart (the grid) and analysed, e.g. by factor analysis, to elucidate the individual's constructs: his view of the world, and of himself in relation to it. This technique is *not* a test; it does not produce norms and is not standardized, being by definition different for each individual. However it can be used to collect normative data for particular purposes. Its advantage is that in some ways it seems the most systematic way of getting close to what a person actually experiences. See Bannister and Fransella, *Inquiring Man* (1971), for a fuller account.

Theories of the self

Theories about the self abound in psychology. The two greatest developmental theorists, Piaget and Freud, both devoted much attention to the ways in which the child gradually comes to be aware of itself as an entity distinct from the environment. Recent experimental research (Korner, 1973) suggests that this may start to happen even earlier than had been thought (see C1, C2, D3). It is perhaps the psychodynamic theorists, deriving from, or influenced by, Freud, who have had most to say about the self, and the way in which one 'self' differs from another. Erik Erikson, for example, accepted Freudian theory, but sought to amplify it by considering the social factors in development. He described the ways in which in the course of childhood each individual seeks his own identity. Particularly at adolescence, a young person 'tries on' various personalities; and it is common observation that adolescents do often adopt standards and manners from a group or another person only, after a time, to throw them over in favour of another set. Successful development involves the emergence of one's own standards. Erikson's account, while stimulating and plausible, is not supported by any substantial body of research; and he does not really tell us why any given individual should develop in that particular way.

In that respect Alfred Adler made more specific statements. Adler originally worked with Freud, but came to disagree with him over the importance of sex as a general basis for behaviour. Adler felt that the origins, or at least the driving force of behaviour, lay in three sources. These were the individual's feelings of inferiority, his striving for superiority, and his desire to contribute to society, or social interest. The first seems to be the original of the popular 'inferiority complex'. Adler's theory was that every human child experiences a period of helpless dependency, and that every human being strives to compensate for this in particular ways in later life. These may take the form of compensation, that is concentrating on areas where one is naturally talented; or over-compensation, striving to excel at things where one is initially weak. Such reactions become co-ordinated in a total life-style, which may as a whole be successful in gaining the individual happiness, or may be self-defeating. As with Freudian theory, the weakness of this is that it can explain almost anything; it is logically impossible to disprove it. Adler did make rather more specific predictions about birth order. A first-born, for example, for a time enjoys a unique position which is lost when a second child is born. Such a child, Adler suggested, will tend to accept and identify with the parents' values. On the other hand a youngest child, always the smallest and weakest in the family, may grow up to be a revolutionary. While this is far from fully investigated, Schachter (1959) did find, for example, a significant tendency for first-borns in one situation to affiliate with – act together with – other people.

A third approach worth mentioning is that of Carl Rogers, who has become well-known as the father of 'non-directive' therapy (see F3). Like Adler, and indeed like Kelly, Rogers believed that what is important for the understanding of behaviour is how an individual perceives the situation he is in. He thought further, however, that no one can fully understand the experiences of another. Rogers postulated that every person has an inbuilt tendency towards 'self-actualization'. This is the tendency to develop all one's capacities in ways which seem to maintain or enhance oneself. Experiences are evaluated as positive or negative insofar as they do or do not contribute to this end. The goal of self-actualization includes not only satisfaction of bodily, or material, or social needs, but also of the need for autonomy and self-determination. Once again the theory, while it clearly predicts that individuals will be very different from each other, does not state what precise differences will result from what particular circumstances. There are some attempts to derive and test hypotheses from the theory. For example Chodorkoff (1954), using Q-sorts, biographical data, and projective tests, found evidence that the greater the agreement between a person's self-description and descriptions of him by others, the better was his personal adjustment. Such studies suggest at least a start in tackling these very complicated problems experimentally.

9
Intellectual differences

In 1904 Charles Spearman sent to the *American Journal of Psychology* an article called 'General intelligence objectively determined and measured'. Here were first clearly stated the essentials of factor analysis. Inspired by the ideas of Galton, Spearman had obtained scores on various items from groups of children, and correlated the results. Using more rigorous and sophisticated techniques than others had done, Spearman concluded that a number of psychological capacities emerged, each involving both a general intellectual factor and another factor specific to that capacity. This was the origin of Spearman's famous 'two factor' theory of intelligence.

Spearman was an unusual man, who spent his early adult life as an officer in the Royal Engineers and was already forty-four when he obtained his first academic appointment. Not his least remarkable characteristic was his belief in the virtues of his own theories, in which, he claimed in 1923: 'The entire range of all cognition whatsoever, as regards both form and material, would appear to receive its definite and final boundaries.' The philosopher's stone that Spearman had discovered consisted of his *noegenetic principles* or laws of creative mind. The basic feature is that the mind, given two objects or ideas, tends to educe, i.e. discover, the relationship between them. Given one idea and a relationship, it tends to educe the correlate. These laws descend from the classical Laws of Association (see A3), but allow for the creation of new ideas. They are still found embodied in intelligence test items of the form: A is to B as C is to ?

General intelligence

The pursuit of 'general intelligence' or 'g' as it came to be known, was carried on by Cyril Burt, who formulated his notion of 'innate, general, cognitive efficiency' as early as 1909, and was still vigorously campaigning for it when he died in 1973 (see Chapter 11). The concept of psychological testing gained a boost during the First World War in both the United States and here. In this country the war produced the Industrial Fatigue Research Board, whose purpose was to increase the efficiency of the wartime work force (see E4 and E5). From this arose the National Institute of Industrial Psychology, which became extremely influential in propagating psychological methods of assessment and diagnosis. It was paralleled by the creation of psychological services in education. Between the two wars, it is fair to say, psychological methods were the new, coming thing; and tests were the psychological methods *par excellence*. The atmosphere was right for the 1944 Education Act; for the employment of psychologists to assess individuals for every sort of career; and for other offshoots such as the creation of Mensa, the society whose members must, to join, score in the top two per cent on a test of 'general intelligence'.

The IQ

Scientific discoveries often resemble pebbles dropped into a pond. By the time the ripples reach the edge, the centre is still again. As 'testing' became a vogue, some psychologists at least were losing the early optimism. Some at least had serious misgivings about the selective system of education that was partly based on their work. Scientific concepts often escape from their creators and pursue a career of their own (a theme that science fiction has reflected since Frankenstein's noble and innocent creation turned into a 'monster'). This happened to the IQ. The Intelligence Quotient, named by Terman in

1916, expresses 'mental age' over chronological age, multiplied by a hundred. Tests are so constructed that, given a normal distribution (Fig. 2.1), the centre point is 100. Psychologists are still asked, by laymen and by others who ought to know better, such as medical practitioners, to give them an individual's IQ. There is no such thing as '*the* IQ'. To begin with different tests have different distributions, just as centigrade and fahrenheit thermometers use different scales. To say the temperature is 50° is meaningless unless we know which scale is being used. Secondly any test, or set of tests, is only a sample of the individual's abilities, which fluctuate over the course of days, let alone years. Thirdly tests are only one aspect of assessment; they can be interpreted only in the light of much other knowledge about the individual. Burt, in his classic work *The Young Delinquent* (1925), listed tests as only one among some dozen sources of information.

Tests undoubtedly lend themselves, even in skilled hands, to abuse. There is the well-known 'self-fulfilling prophecy'. Selection or rejection for particular sorts of schooling or work may itself contribute to success or failure. Human beings are remarkably adaptable: to a large degree they will produce the behaviour demanded by the situation. As we have stressed, tests and assessments are products of a particular culture; and so is the concept of intelligence, which has most often been at the centre of attempts to measure intellectual abilities.

Defining intelligence

Possibly more words have been used in trying to define intelligence than for any other psychological concept. We shall not add to the list. The attempts fall roughly into three groups. Early definitions were intuitive: they were merely assertions that intelligence 'is' the ability to learn, or solve problems, or what not. Then, secondly, there are logical or philosophical attempts, of which probably the most famous is that of Gilbert Ryle in *The Concept of Mind* (1949). Perhaps the essence of his message was that 'intelligence' is not an entity, a sort of engine inside the man causing him to act in certain ways. Nor yet is it certain sorts of behaviour. Rather, any action can be

61

done intelligently or stupidly. When we say that an individual is intelligent, we mean that he characteristically acts in intelligent ways in all, or many of, the things he does. And what *that* means is that, for example, he acts with regard to the consequences; he is able to adapt to changes in the situation, innovating where necessary; that he acts in ways that are logically related to the ends he wishes to attain.

The structure of intellect

Ryle's approach, of course, is not so much an analysis of what intelligence 'is', as of what we are talking about when we use the word. On the whole, psychologists have preferred to take the third of the approaches to defining intelligence, an empirical/theoretical one: to start from some assumptions about what is important, to collect scores over a range of performances, factor analyse these, and construct a theoretical framework to accommodate the results. The main division of opinion here is between those who favour some general factor and those who prefer to conceive of a number of separate factors. L. L. Thurstone (1938) for example felt that the evidence justified seven 'primary mental abilities': spatial ability; perceptual speed; numerical ability; memory; verbal meaning; verbal fluency; inductive reasoning. The most elaborate set of factors is that devised by J. P. Guilford and his co-workers. Guilford begins by arguing that any account of intellectual abilities must deal with three classes of variables: the activities or operations performed; the material or content on which operations are performed; and the product which is the result of operations. There are said to be, respectively, five, four, and six items in each class, and this yields a total of $4 \times 5 \times 6 = 120$ mental factors. Thus, for example, the operation 'memory' can be performed on any of four sorts of content, in each case yielding one of six possible products. It is then a case of seeing whether empirical investigations yield evidence for the predicted factors; and the answer (e.g. Guilford and Hoepfner, 1966) is that they do so well for some, less well for others. While easily the most elaborate account, Guilford's *structure of intellect*, as it is known, has perhaps been less generally useful for practical purposes than the broader factors of Thurstone or Burt.

Burt's hierarchical system
Burt takes his stand on several grounds: statistical, empirical, logical, and common-sensical. Since he was engaged in piling up evidence for some sixty years, we can mention only a few

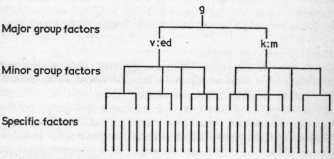

g = general intelligence
v:ed = verbal–educational ability
k:m = spatial–mechanical ability

After Vernon (1950) *The Structure of Human Abilities* Methuen.

Fig. 9.1

This diagram suggests the way intellectual abilities might be organized hierarchically. It should not be thought that just this number of factors, in just this arrangement, have been established.

aspects here. Burt argues that when an individual is assessed on any one of a set of characteristics, the result must be a function of four kinds of components: those common to all the characteristics or traits; those common to some; those unique to the particular trait whenever it is measured; and those unique to this particular trait as measured on this particular occasion. This analysis yields a hierarchical model of general, group, specific factors (see Fig. 9.1). (Components unique to the particular occasion do not, of course, yield factors.)

63

Burt argued for a hierarchical system also on the basis that the brain and nervous system appeared to be thus organized from the researches of Sir Charles Sherrington around the turn of the century (see A2). From a practical point of view such a system may be the most useful since, as Butcher (1968) argues, measurement of a general factor allows prediction over a wider range of situations. Butcher likewise claims that this approach explains how some earlier results seemed contradictory. They caused confusion by making comparisons between supposed factors at different levels in the hierarchy.

Heredity and environment

Burt's massive researches left him convinced of the reality and usefulness of a concept of general intelligence or, as he defined it, 'innate general cognitive ability'. His defence of this definition is based partly on the evidence; and partly on the fact that, historically, this is how the term has often been used. Burt also paid a great deal of attention to the origins of intellectual ability, and felt able to attribute it approximately 80 per cent to heredity and 20 per cent to environment. The arguments for this are highly technical, involving the amounts of variance accounted for by sets of variables (see Chapter 12). However, it is possible to criticize the conclusion on rather simpler grounds, namely that to speak of 'an innate ability' makes no sense; the only thing that could be innate would be the *potential to develop* an ability. This is approximately the line taken by D. O. Hebb (1949) in a book that influenced much of psychology for several years, *The Organization of Behaviour*. Publishing in the same year as Ryle, Hebb came out firmly for intelligence as a causal factor in behaviour. This seems based on confusion, but Hebb did distinguish usefully between what he termed *Intelligence A* which is innate potential, the capacity for development; and *Intelligence B* which is 'the functioning of a brain in which development has gone on'. Throughout his writings Hebb constantly gets muddled about the relationship of physiology to behaviour (see A2); but he was right to argue that Intelligence A cannot be measured directly; our evidence for it must come through

Intelligence B. Vernon (1969) has taken a further step and pointed out that, in fact, all we can do is take a *sample* of Intelligence B, which he calls Intelligence C.

A biological viewpoint
In contrast to both the philosophical and psychometric approaches to the problem there stands the biological viewpoint of Piaget, based on a body of research far too vast to summarize (see C1, C2). Piaget considers intellectual growth to be analogous with physical development inasmuch as an organism is a structured entity in continual interaction with the environment. What is taken from the environment – food, for example, or information – is incorporated into the organism which thereby develops more complex structures. 'Intelligence' refers to the balancing and regulating process involved in interaction, which itself becomes ever more complex in the course of development. (Attempts to put Piagetian concepts into a few words have led to more than a little bafflement, and we are well aware that we may be worsening the situation. For a longer attempt, see Radford and Burton, 1974.)

Can intelligence be increased?
This viewpoint, though based on different grounds, does seem consistent with a notion of intellectual abilities as modes of functioning in diverse environments. To some, it has seemed to indicate that abilities could be dramatically increased, if only we provided the optimal intellectual nutrition. J. McV. Hunt (1961) for example, launched a somewhat polemical attack on the theory, which he held to have been dominant, of the fixed and unalterable nature of intelligence. Quoting many instances of variability even on standardized tests, he concluded that in an adequately planned environment children would develop substantially faster, and the level of adult intellectual functioning would be substantially higher, than now. The argument is logically faulty: it is rather like saying that because we know roses grow at different rates, and that manure is good for them, we can get all rose bushes to bloom

65

earlier and better. Horticulturists know that limits are set by the nature of the stock, which can only be substantially altered by breeding. This conclusion is a risky one for human capacities, however, since as we have stressed (p. 17) these are by definition reflexive. A man is cleverer than us if he does things we cannot – solve problems, for example. But problems are problems only because human beings so classify them. What would it mean to say that average intelligence was raised?

In the meantime, testing and theorizing go on. Despite Hudson's critique (p. 47) tests are of definite, if circumscribed, use in providing information. The new British Intelligence Scale presently under construction, using a technique called Rasch scaling, promises to give us an intellectual profile of an individual rather than a thermometer reading. H. J. Eysenck is engaged on a sophisticated research programme designed to establish what he believes to be the three major components of intelligence. He points out that when people tackle problems, they do so in a variety of different ways. These can be analysed into three factors: the speed with which solutions are reached; the accuracy of the solutions (many or few errors); and the degree of persistence shown when problems prove difficult. Furthermore these differences may vary from problem to problem. To get a complete picture of intelligence, it is necessary to measure each of the component factors accurately on each of a series of problems; and, of course, to take an extensive range of subjects. This can only be done using quite complex apparatus and computer analysis. If Eysenck is right, this could lead to the first major new development in the theory of intellectual abilities since the early days of factor analysis.

10
Creativity

American usage groups together as 'exceptional' those individuals with special gifts and those with handicaps. The latter are dealt with elsewhere in this series (F2). Here we are concerned with intellectual giftedness in particular. In the heyday of intelligence testing it may have appeared to some that this was simply a matter of coming at the far upper end of a normal distribution. Galton, investigating hereditary genius, made no such mistake, since he was concerned with the eminent and productive individual. After him, however, the study of creativity, as distinct from the ability to obtain very high IQ scores, languished (see A7). It came dramatically back into favour in the 1950s and 60s, partly due to the 'Cold War' and the wish of the Great Powers to find and develop the scientific and technological gifts of their citizens. The Russian city of Novosibirsk, a sort of scientific nursery, has become widely if vaguely known and there are others; while in the United States training courses and techniques promising to develop creative thought flourish by the score.

The analysis of creativity
The boom can be dated to a famous Presidential address to the American Psychological Association in 1950 by J. P. Guilford. As part of his comprehensive analysis of intellectual activities

(p. 62) Guilford was concerned with the ability to produce new ideas. He concluded eventually that six or so of his 120 factors were particularly important. In 1950, however, he wished to stress the limitations of the conventional intelligence test. In this, there is always one right answer; any other response, however ingenious, counts for nothing. To this distinction the words 'convergent' and 'divergent' became attached. In Guilford's system, these are just two of the five *operations* (see p. 62); they may or may not be involved in creative thinking. As so often, however, a popular version of a complex theory developed, in which divergent thought is creative, and convergent not. And this has come to have almost a moral tone, so that divergent thought is good and must be encouraged; convergence is the mark of the bad, the old, the reactionary, etc. A moment's reflection, to say nothing of research, makes it obvious that in many areas, such as mathematics, creativity does precisely involve finding the one right answer. Merton (1961) has shown that many highly creative persons are distinguished *not* by the vast number of novel ideas they have, but by the fact that a very high proportion of the ideas they *do* have are good ones. Indeed, nothing is easier than novelty. A computer can produce new ideas by simply running through all possible combinations of a set of variables. But which are the good ones?

Tests of creativity
Nevertheless on this basis 'tests of creativity' appeared, and some have become famous. One often-used item is 'uses for objects': list as many uses for a brick or a bucket as possible in a given period. Another test presents the recipient with a title, and calls for stories or pictures to be made about it. Probably the most extensive set has been devised by E. P. Torrance at the University of Minnesota. Based originally on Guilford's theory, they include such items as: drawing as many items as possible using a basic circle shape; thinking of improvements to a toy monkey or dog; listing as many impossible things as one can; listing problems that might arise in a common situation, such as taking a bath.

The obvious difficulty with such tests lies in establishing their reliability and still more their validity. Goldman (1967), reviewing work on the Minnesota tests, in fact reports some quite high scores for reliability. Validity is another matter, and Goldman reports no findings here that are at all convincing. The first problem is clearly what the tests are to be validated *against*: as Vernon (1964) points out, it is little use for tests to produce a flow of novel responses, or what not, unless it can be shown that they discriminate between individuals known on *other* grounds to be creative. And for this, satisfactory evidence is lacking (Yamamoto, 1965).

Attempts to test have given rise, however, to some of the best known and influential studies of creativity including those of Getzels and Jackson (1962); Hudson (1966, 1968); and Wallach and Kogan (1965). Getzels and Jackson studied 449 adolescents from a mid-Western school in the United States, of generally above average intelligence. Using a standard intelligence test and five 'creativity' measures, they selected two smaller groups for further study: one of those in the top 20 per cent for creativity but below that level on IQ; the other vice versa. The general tenor of their report was that the highly creative subjects were less conventional, less liked by teachers, had a more obvious sense of humour, were less suited to the school system. This tended to reinforce the notion of two sorts of able person, the convergent and the divergent. Actually the study is very selective and inconclusive, as was pointed out by Cyril Burt in a masterly review. It is true that when correlations are calculated between tests of intelligence and tests of creativity, the coefficients tend to be very low – of the order of $+0\cdot10$ or $+0\cdot20$ (Torrance, 1967, collating 178 such correlations). However the most likely relationship is that in order to be creative some minimum level of intelligence, above average but differing with the area of activity, is normally necessary. Beyond that, other factors are more important (Barron, 1969).

Wallach and Kogan stressed, among other points, that creative ability might not emerge in an atmosphere of school and 'tests'. They got teachers, accordingly, to incorporate measures of creativity into the normal lessons and games. They felt able to distinguish four types of children: high/low intelligence combined with high/low creativity. Really, these were four styles of dealing with the school environment rather than just abilities; and this rather broader approach is supported by Hudson. His subjects were potential university students, boys aged 14–18 in grammar and public schools in this country. This is a highly specialized sample; nevertheless Hudson's findings are of general interest. He agrees with the unsatisfactoriness of tests of creativity, and also with the relationship to intelligence tests suggested above. Likewise, he rejects the over-simplification that divergers are creative, convergers not. What Hudson argues is that the most important factors are personal, not intellectual; and this he has illustrated with some ingenious experiments. For example, he has had boys respond to, say, a 'uses of objects' test as they think someone else would: either 'Higgins', a conventional engineer, or 'McMice', a bohemian artist. The differences are startling: it looks almost as if virtually anyone, given the opportunity, *could* be convergent or divergent as appropriate. Of course it would be a big jump to conclude that anyone could be really creative.

Personal qualities

Hudson considers the central focus of the important personal qualities to be the *sense of identity*. The individual in a sense decides what he is going to be, and this regulates his reactions to the environment, his patterns of behaviour, his use of his capacities. This view is supported by several studies showing that creative persons tend to have well-developed, definite personalities. MacKinnon (1960) summarizes this very well:

The truly creative individual has an image of himself as a responsible person and a sense of destiny about himself as a human being. This includes a degree of resoluteness and almost inevitably a measure of egotism. But over and above these, there is a belief in the foregone certainty of the worth and validity of one's creative efforts.

70

This is very neat, but as with almost every psychological finding one can at once think of exceptions: George Eliot, for example, who saw little worth in her own novels; James Boswell, vacillating from one authority figure to another; Thomas Gray, famous for his poems, when appointed Regius Professor of History at Oxford, lacked the confidence ever to give his first lecture.

And even if the picture of personal qualities is broadly true, it does not explain how creative activity comes about. Hudson's explanation is one he terms 'existential'. The intellectually creative individual, he thinks, seeks to involve himself in crises in which his own identity, the integrity of his personality, is at stake. He plunges, as it were, so deeply into his creative work that he risks not emerging as the independent individual he was. This Hudson relates to the primitive wish of an infant to be totally engulfed by someone else, namely the mother. Actually, this wish, balanced by the desire to become autonomous, was explored in detail by Melanie Klein, who derived her inspiration from psychoanalysis rather than existentialism.

Unconscious processes

Certainly it seems that at least one vital part of the explanation of creative thought must lie in factors that are 'unconscious'. At the simplest, it is quite clear that creative persons cannot say how they come by their good ideas. Ghiselin (1952) collected autobiographical accounts; Wertheimer (1945) reported a long series of conversations with Einstein. While there may in some cases be conditions in which individuals work best (although Johnson maintained stoutly: 'A man may write at any time, if he will set himself doggedly to it'), what cannot be discovered by introspection is where the new ideas come from and how they are recognized as good. Conversely, there are famous anecdotes of creative ideas arising through dreams or reverie (Kekulé and the benzene ring, Coleridge and *Kubla Khan*, for example, see Ghiselin, 1952). Psychoanalysis has described mechanisms of a kind that might be involved in novelty of thought, such as sublimation, displacement, and condensation (see D3). Many writers agree that creative thought often involves seeing similarities where these had not been seen before; regrouping or restructuring of ideas. The apparently flexible, bizarre, and image-borne nature of 'unconscious' thought processes could be important.

Accordingly psychoanalytic writers on creativity, e.g. Kris (1952), often stress the value of 'regression in the service of the ego'; allowing oneself to explore feelings and motives normally hidden, to express oneself in ways usually thought childish. This, indeed, could be one source of the popular belief that genius is next to madness. Another, simpler one is that geniuses tend to have ideas which are not comprehended by most people. Many writers, such as Colin Wilson (*The Outsider*, 1956) and Donald Schon (1963), have favoured the concept of the creative individual as a lonely, romantic revolutionary, isolated from society, seeking some ideal with utter dedication. In line with the supposed role of the unconscious, means of uncovering this, which are also favoured by the romantic outsider, are claimed to increase creativity: drugs, meditation, trance states. There is very little firm evidence here. The creativity claimed is often of the vaguest kind, often amounting to some kind of personal satisfaction which, however desirable, may have nothing to do with creative production. One thing that seems clear is that the effects of such techniques depend heavily upon the individual personality and the whole social setting in which they are used (Wells, 1973).

Creativity and technique
In fact, while creative thought may well involve unconscious processes, there has perhaps been too great an emphasis on the spontaneous and the unstructured, possibly in reaction against the rather restricted society in which we live (see D1). Creativity in many areas certainly depends also on sheer hard work – Edison's 99 per cent perspiration. More than this: it depends upon, arises out of, mastery of techniques. Technique alone will not produce an insightful solution or a new work of great art, but it will often do quite well until that comes along. The more important point, though, is that it is the actual *mastery* of technique that enables the creative work to exist. The

creative person is very frequently dedicated to his technique; consider the lifelong self-discipline of ballet dancers or of artists such as Hokusai. This must tend to produce a unique personality in ways which as yet we hardly understand.

Actually, 'creative' is a very ill-defined term. Taylor (1959) attempted to sort out some of the confusion by distinguishing different *levels* of creative thinking, from that of free, unstructured play to that of fundamentally new advances in abstract thinking. Almost certainly a host of dimensions is involved, along which individuals may vary.

Improving creativity

It is natural to ask whether geniuses are born or made; and as usual the answer is probably no. Creative work at any of Taylor's levels has to be the outcome of a complex interaction. Attempts to improve creativity are hard to evaluate. So-called 'creative education' usually boils down to having the children walk about instead of sit still, make glove puppets instead of doing sums, and not bother too much about spelling. Making adults more creative often depends on starting with engineers or businessmen for whom a little free speculation may well be a useful corrective to their important but convergent training. Rarely does this sort of work tackle any more fundamental problem; and many a gimmick has become commercially profitable while being little more than yet another redescription of 'insight' or what not. One more interesting effort, called *synectics* (the joining together of diverse elements), seeks deliberately to employ the sort of thinking based on analogies believed to be involved in both unconscious processes and scientific discovery.

It is widely accepted that certain cultures have been more creative in some sense than others. They have been marked by significant advances in philosophy or science, by enduring achievements in the arts. While the brilliance of classical Greece or renaissance Europe may blind us to the achievements of more static societies, it is plausible to think that, given appropriate conditions, individuals can be occasioned to rise to new heights. What these conditions are, is far from known:

see Radford and Burton (1974) for a discussion. Just to hint at the complexity, we might mention the well-known (though unfair) comment that sixteenth-century Italy was a land of pestilence, war, and civil disorder, and produced Leonardo da Vinci; Switzerland on the other hand has enjoyed three hundred years of uninterrupted peace, and has produced the cuckoo-clock.

II
Sir Cyril Burt

> Were I to apply my own methods of case study to myself, I should follow my favourite scheme: to start with my family history, and to look first for evidence of heredity to account for my numerous abilities and foibles, and then turn to environmental influences. (Burt, 1962)

Sir Cyril Burt was born on 3 March 1883, the son of a physician. His family were very interested themselves in the effects of heredity on personality, and he absorbed this along with an excellent general education. His parents were highly cultured with a knowledge of literature, art, music, architecture. Burt's own hobbies as a boy were collecting natural history specimens, and practical chemistry. Burt won a scholarship to public school (Christ's Hospital) and later to Oxford – turning down an Exhibition at Cambridge.

He accompanied his father a good deal on the latter's visits. Burt's father, as it happened, was physician to Darwin Galton, then an ailing old man, who was the father of Francis Galton. The latter was impressed upon Cyril Burt by his father as an ideal man. When, as a schoolboy, Burt discovered from the flyleaf of Galton's *Inquiries into Human Faculty* that it had been published in the year of his own birth, it gave him a 'superstitious thrill'.

At Oxford he wished to take medicine but he was told that since his scholarship was in classics that was what he must study. He did, however, acquire a knowledge of philosophy, and attended lectures in anthropology. From these he went to physiology, and there met William McDougall (see D1). Burt quickly resolved to take a psychological special subject for finals – the standardization of tests. The demand for psychology was so small that for a time he was McDougall's only student. Burt about now purchased the first volume of *Biometrika*, a new journal just founded by Galton. He met Pearson and Spearman, and all three worked on the theory of correlation and multiple correlation, subsequently to become factor analysis. In 1909 Burt began to calculate 'index characters' for intellectual differences. In this year he published his first scientific paper, beginning it:

> The experimental determination of the mental characters of individuals is admittedly a problem of wide theoretical interest and of vast practical importance. The particular mental character which in importance is above all supreme, is that traditionally termed 'General Intelligence'.

As Hearnshaw (1964) remarks, no one could accuse Burt of beating about the bush. The editor of the new British Journal of Psychology, however, regretted that Burt 'had devoted so much time and industry to a transient problem, like mental testing, which holds so little promise for the future'.

Burt spent some time at Würzburg with Külpe, who was engaged in the systematic introspection of thought processes. Then he took a post in Sherrington's physiology department at Liverpool, where he taught psychology to medical students. Later he commented: ' . . . with the vanity of youth I felt it was upon me to make the most of the revolutionary views which I felt psychological studies would introduce.'

For those who may have thought of Burt as a strict hereditarian, or even a racist, it is interesting to note that, so important did he think the effects of environment that he chose to live in slum areas so as to gain understanding of problem cases. Thus he received a training in 'practical sociology'. In 1913 he became the first British educational psychologist, joining the school inspectorate of the London County Council. He surveyed and visited schools, studying normals, subnormals, and supernormals, employing multivariate analysis and numerous other techniques. Again he lived in slums and spent weekends with a docker, with costers and a burglar (on a back street off the Seven Sisters Road, Holloway). Determined to follow up his young delinquents in their post-school careers, Burt at one time got himself accepted as a presumable member of a criminal gang that planned its activities in a disreputable little Soho restaurant. 'As I am a born Londoner, I could drop into Cockney and understand the idiom and the background. You must have shared the cultural background of a child to appreciate it.'

In World War I Burt became Secretary to the Psychology Committee on War Research Problems. Through most of his career Burt was active and effective in committee work, which is where so many educational and other policies are determined. In 1919 when C. S. Myers established the National Institute of Industrial Psychology, Burt became (part-time) head of the Vocational Guidance Department. More surprisingly, he was one of the small group who founded the British Psycho-analytic Society, which sought to propagate Freud's still revolutionary ideas, and to arouse interest in potentially neurotic children.

In 1926 Burt accepted the Chair of Educational Psychology at the London Day Training Centre, now the University of London Institute of Education. Then from 1931 to 1951 he held the Chair of Psychology at University College, London. In both posts, he continued his clinical work as well as writing and teaching. His main aim in the U.C.L. Chair was:

to preserve its original traditions, and to make it a focus for that branch of psychology which was founded and developed by Galton: 'individual' psychology or as Stern puts it, 'differential psychology', the study of the mental differences between individuals, sexes, social classes, and other groups.

In his retirement Burt continued to be almost as academically active as before, writing with his usual grasp and enthusiasm until shortly before his death in 1973. In his last years, however, he undertook no public engagements due partly to increasing deafness.

The major focus of Burt's work was, of course, intelligence and its analysis. Unlike Spearman, he did not regard factors as causal agents: they were 'principles of classification', a convenient and exact means of description with many useful purposes such as prediction and the elucidation of origins. Burt's view was that intellectual performance could be attributed to both hereditary and environmental factors, the former being of more importance. This relationship could be expressed numerically, viz. 80 per cent to 20 per cent. The worth of this argument depends partly upon what sort of question it is useful to ask, and partly upon the evidence and the statistics. Burt is best known for this view, but as we have stressed this in no way made him neglect environmental factors. Nor did he limit himself to intelligence. In 1915 he reported an investigation into the 'General and specific factors underlying the primary emotions'. Later studies produced a normally distributed factor which foreshadowed quite closely Eysenck's introversion–extraversion dimension. Eysenck has also pursued another of Burt's interests, aesthetic taste.

12
The nature–nurture controversy

Gregor Mendel, an Austrian monk who studied the inheritance of certain traits in peas about a hundred years ago, was the first to demonstrate two fundamental principles of genetics (see C1). One is that traits are transmitted as discrete particles which do not contaminate or blend with each other; the other is that two traits, considered simultaneously, will sort and recombine independently of each other. This puts paid to the notion of inheritance as a kind of 'mixing of blood'. Modern molecular genetics seeks to uncover the mechanisms underlying Mendel's laws. The units of heredity are now known to be *genes* (which are large molecules of deoxyribonucleic acid). Genes occur in pairs, and are situated on *chomosomes*, which are structures within living cells. It is known that there are forty-six pairs of chromosomes in human cells, and estimated that there may be 1,000 genes per chromosome. Each cell has an identical set, which is to say that the heredity of every cell is the same.

Mendel's work was not known to Galton who, however, (in contrast to Darwin) was thinking on similar lines. Genetics seems to offer the possibility of solving the problem that has been continually posed since Galton: to what extent are human psychological characteristics the product of inheritance, and to what extent of environment? (See C1.) Although this question applies to all human characteristics, in practice far the greatest concentration has been on intelligence. In general there are probably three main attitudes to the question: it is impossible of solution; it is possible to solve but unimportant; it is both possible and important.

Heredity and environment

The problem has been greatly confused by difficulties over what is meant by the concepts of heredity and environment. When human beings reproduce, the chromosome pairs split into two on a random basis in each reproductive cell. The new organism receives a random selection of half the chromosomes from each parent. This yields an extremely large number of new gene combinations; and since even the simplest human characteristics depend upon the combined effect of a large number of genes, the possibilities for inherited variability are immense. The particular set of genes received is really all that can be meant by 'heredity'. Anything that occurs from the moment of fertilization on is environmental. (Actually, even the nature of the genes can be altered – mutated – by some environmental circumstances such as radiation.) It is apparent that environment, therefore, includes the situation in which the genes find themselves, viz. the cytoplasm of the cell. It also includes that which surrounds each cell, i.e. other cells. It includes the prenatal conditions of the developing organism, and then all that happens after birth. The possibilities are thus already infinite, but are further multiplied by other factors. Any organism determines its own environment, since it interacts selectively with the available range of stimuli. Even very simple organisms will respond variously to identical stimuli, while at the human end of the scale there is no logical way to equate the experience of one individual with that of another. Moreover, it is known that a given environmental factor can interact differently with different specific types of hereditary material. For example (and a relatively simple one) a rise in temperature affects the number of eye facets in the fruit fly *Drosophila*. But identical changes in temperature have different effects upon flies having different gene constitutions.

Thus it should be clear that even from a genetic point of view there can be no way of determining that characteristics are the result of heredity *or* environment. They can only be the outcome of a complex interaction, and one which is specific to the population studied. In fact, it is unique to the individual. Apart from identical twins (see below) the chances of two individuals having the same genetic constitution are almost infinitely small; but even identical twins cannot logically have identical environments, since they cannot occupy the same position in space.

Empirical investigations
Logical difficulties should not deter science, however, and it is possible to attack empirically the problem of the relative contributions of heredity and environment. Anastasi (1958) lists five approaches. These are: selective breeding; normative developmental studies; structural factors in behavioural development; the effects of prior experience upon behaviour; and studies of family resemblances.

Galton advocated *selective breeding*, not so much for research as to raise the level of the race; his Eugenics Society still exists, but fosters conferences rather than controlled mating. It is certainly possible to breed successfully for psychological characteristics in non-human species. Tryon (1940) produced strains of rats particularly good at running mazes. A more sophisticated development is known as behaviour genetics or psychogenetics and dates from the work of Fuller and Thompson (1960). It has served to emphasize the complexity of the issues rather than resolve them. The early work of Broadhurst (1963), for example, indicates that psychological traits are controlled by many genes – up to one hundred in the case of emotional reactivity, for instance. Broadhurst points out that each of these may respond uniquely to any environmental change.

Studies of the normal course of development can suggest the relative roles of heredity and environment. If any behaviour typically appears suddenly, apparently without the need for learning, clearly heredity is indicated. If a sequence of behaviour normally or always appears in a fixed pattern, the same conclusion follows. Most work here has concentrated on relatively simple sensori-motor functions such as walking or crying; and in many cases these do appear to be unlearned. But apart from the fact that these are of lesser interest psychologically, the argument is a weak one. We do not know what experience might actually be important – possibly visual stimuli. There is evidence, for example, that blind babies do smile, but subsequently this drops out (Freedman, 1964). Again, those infants who have been observed to develop walking in a uniform manner have generally been reared in rather uniform environments.

Similarly, studies of structural factors do not go very far to resolving the nature–nurture issue. It is possible to show, for example, how particular developments in the brain and nervous system are necessary conditions for normal functioning. But, presumably, structure and function develop together as the result of the interaction of heredity and environment.

Development under special conditions
The fourth approach is in some ways more interesting, if not necessarily more conclusive. It is possible to subject young animals, and to a lesser extent young humans, to *special conditions* in order to see whether normal development is affected. If not, it is argued, heredity must be at work. This suffers from the same objection as the second method, that we do not know what the important variables are. Some of the findings, however, are at least suggestive. For example, female rats reared in cages containing nothing that could be picked up or carried failed to make nests when materials were provided. Nor did they, as is normal, gather their young together into a single area (Riess, 1954). Several well-known attempts have been made to get chimpanzees to acquire human-type abilities. The Kelloggs with *Gua*, and the Hayes with *Viki*, both achieved some success, indicating that environment can at least modify normal development. A more dramatic case is that of *Sarah*, reported by Premack (1972). He concentrated on language, and in order to overcome the chimpanzee's lack

of vocal apparatus, used symbols placed on a magnetic board. Sarah, it was claimed, could understand and even construct sentences. Equally spectacular results have been reported by the Gardners (1969) using sign language.

The converse of this is when human infants are reared by animals. So-called 'feral' children are obviously hard to investigate. Zingg (1940) surveyed most of the known cases, over forty of them, many of which are merely anecdotal. On discovery, such children typically lack the basics of human culture: language, social consciousness and behaviour, overt emotion. They do not wear clothes, do not cook food. Often they have animal forms of behaviour such as running on all fours, smelling food before eating, sharpening teeth on bones. On return to human society, in some cases at least the child may acquire human behaviour and lead a relatively normal existence. Others do not survive long. One great difficulty, of course, is to know what the child was like originally. It might have been mentally deficient or otherwise abnormal, and this might have been the cause of its being abandoned. In so far as they suggest anything, it is the necessity of normal human interaction.

The last group of investigations include those on which greatest weight has been placed. There are two varieties. One method is to trace *human pedigrees* or family trees. Galton used a version of this; and some of the other examples have become famous, notably the Jukes, and the Kallikaks. The latter, described by Goddard (1912), who imported the Binet test to America, stemmed from one Martin Kallikak who at the time of the American Revolution gave rise to two sets of descendants: one through an illegitimate child by a feeble-minded girl, the other through his wife, a woman of intelligence and good family. One set was composed largely of defectives, the other of worthy and eminent citizens. Such, Goddard held, were the effects of 'bad blood'. The reader may care to count the flaws in the argument.

The other way is to compare statistically individuals having varying degrees of *family resemblance*. The most general finding is that, the closer the family, i.e. genetic, relationship, the higher the degree of similarity on any of a number of psychological characteristics. For example, Erlenmayer-Kimling and Jarvik (1963) collected correlation coefficients for intelligence test scores from about one hundred groups (Fig. 12.1).

Category		0·00	0·10	0·20	0·30	0·40	0·50	0·60	0·70	0·80	0·90	Groups included
Unrelated persons	Reared apart											4
	Reared together											5
Fosterparent — child												3
Parent — child												12
Siblings	Reared apart											2
	Reared together											35
Twins — Two-egg	Opposite sex											9
	Like sex											11
Twins — One-egg	Reared apart											4
	Reared together											14

Fig. 12.1 *Correlation coefficients for intelligence test scores from 52 studies.* (From L. Erlenmeyer-Kimling and L. F. Jarvik (1963) Genetics and intelligence: A review, *Science 142*: 1477–1479. Copyright 1963 by the American Association for the Advancement of Science.) Vertical lines represent median scores, while horizontal indicate the ranges.

Twin studies

The best controlled case of relationship is that of identical twins, as Galton was, once again, the first to see. About one quarter of all twins derive from a single fertilized ovum. This means that they have identical genetic constitutions and thus here we have the only opportunity of keeping one side of the equation constant. Burt made considerable use of data from twins, reporting in 1966 results very similar to those in Fig. 12.1 He says: 'The outstanding feature of my results is the high correlation for IQ between identical twins reared apart: 0·87 as compared with 0·55 for fraternal twins reared together.' From such data (using a statistical method of partitioning the sources of variance in a variable) Burt devised his famous conclusion of 80 per cent inherited, 20 per cent environmental.

Some of the arguments about twin and relationship studies are statistical and we shall not embark on them. But some other points can be mentioned. Many early studies were ignorant of the fact that the identification of identical twins is, in fact, quite difficult. However, given reasonable certainty, there is next the fact that twins are genetically not typical of the population as a whole. It is not at present possible to say how serious this is. The next problem is the old one of the environment. There is no way of being certain that the environments of identical twins reared apart are more different than those of fraternal twins reared together. By virtue of their identity they may call forth responses, or select stimuli from their surroundings, which constitute for them a very similar experience.

Again, it could be argued that the data of Erlenmayer-Kimling and Jarvik equally show a significant effect of the environment; for even unrelated persons reared together correlate 0·3. Such objections however do not mean that Burt was wrong in his attempt to partition the variance between different sources, at least with reference to specified populations. Cattell has presented an even more sophisticated attempt. Consider the variation in intelligence in a given population. This can be divided into variation *between* families (related groups) and that *within* families. Each of these in turn includes an environmental and a hereditary element, giving four sources of variance. But any pair of these may be correlated, yielding six further sources of variance. Cattell's technique of Multiple Abstract Variance Analysis attempts to deal with such complexities.

If such problems are overcome, it is possible to attribute values to sources of variation within a population. It is *not* possible to say for an individual how much of his intelligence, or any trait, is inherited or otherwise. It is not possible to partition the variance in a sample of one. Nor is it legitimate to speak of fixed environmental or hereditary components of intelligence as such: to say that 'intelligence *is* x per cent inherited'.

Galton argued that intelligence was largely inherited, and this view has tended to be popular with psychometricians. J. B. Watson, the founder of behaviourism, on the other hand, declared that he could make of any child what he chose.

Opinions on this matter, even among psychologists, have too often been a matter of faith rather than evidence. The controversy seems to have some special quality which causes participants to abandon reason. The extremes of fanaticism are seen in Hitler's fantastic and paranoid murder of six million Jews in an attempt to destroy the entire race. Contemporary China, in line with communist dogma, insists upon the opposite view.

13
Differences between races

The study of racial differences suffers from the usual problems attendant upon the study of group differences. But it also suffers intensely from political and ideological issues, which have been brought to fever pitch in recent years by arguments over whether some groups are more or less intelligent than others, and if so, whether the cause lies in heredity or environment. To some, the attempt to investigate this scientifically has seemed to be part of an attempt to justify prejudice and oppression. To some it even seems that if a difference were shown to be hereditary, this must be denied or suppressed – violently if necessary.

Psychology tries to be a science. This means that it tries to discover what is the case, to pursue its discoveries into the origins and causes of what it discovers, and to carry them forward into predictions of what will be the case. In this sense it tries to be objective and truthful – to show things as they are. There are good grounds for supposing that while this aim can never be absolutely fulfilled, we can hope to approximate to the truth. At the same time it is now widely conceded that scientific research has a strong component of subjectivity. One highly relevant instance is the fact that for every set of data or explicanda (things to be explained) there may well be an indefinite number of explanations which fit. The one selected is chosen for aesthetic, emotional, and economic reasons. It is not chosen for 'scientific' reasons. This applies as much to anti-racists as to allegedly 'racist' scientists.

The concept of race

The concept of race is a confused one. In popular use, it generally refers to a discriminable group to which the speaker can identify himself as belonging or not belonging. The belief is that members of the group share a common heredity (though one hears of 'the black race' in which the most diverse coloured groups are included). It is certainly best to restrict the concept to a biological meaning, namely the genetic differentiation of populations. A 'race' is a reproductive community sharing a common gene pool. But such pools overlap: it is only a *preponderance* of genetic characteristics that differentiates one population from another. And from this it follows that the definition of a race is arbitrary: all members of *homo sapiens* share a very large number of genetic characteristics. It is not even known at what point in evolution different branches began to appear – whether it was before or after we emerged as a distinct species.

Garn (1961) has sought to bring order into the confusion by defining three kinds of Mendelian (genetic) populations or races: geographical, local, and micro-geographical or micro-races. The largest unit is a population confined within a *geographical area*. An example is the Amerindians, which range from Alaska to Tierra del Fuego, and have, among other things, low incidence of the genes for type B blood. Other such major groups are: Polynesian, Micronesian, Melanesian-Papuan, Australian, Asiatic, Indian, European, African. *Local* races are, approximately, breeding populations within a geographical race, separated by physical or social obstacles. They number in the hundreds and include typical cultural groups distinguished by social anthropologists: Eskimo, Navajo, Bantu, Basques, Gypsies. The smallest units are '*significant pockets of variation*' (Gottesman) and may be the result of assortative mating, e.g. in the old Scottish clan system, or of local environmental conditions, especially in preindustrial societies of low mobility. Gottesman reports distinct micro-races, differing by blood-group genes, in Wales.

Human races are not pure: they are mobile, and they can and do interbreed. Taking the case of the coloured population of the United States, even setting aside those of Amerindian descent, we find a hybrid group, a mixture of African and Afro-American stock. Eysenck (1971) reports that the best available estimates suggest an admixture of about 25–30 per cent white genes in present-day Negroes in the USA. But here too there are local variations. Pollitzer (1958) concentrated on US Negroes living near the former great importation centre for slaves, Charleston. He used both fifteen serological (blood) characteristics and nine morphological (appearance) characteristics. This illustrates the partly arbitrary nature of the identification of race, since other characteristics could have been used. Pollitzer found, however, that the Charleston Negroes are, genetically, much more like their West African forefathers than are those living further north.

Thus it is possible to distinguish races meaningfully if arbitrarily. The psychologist wishes to know whether there are *behavioural* differences between such groups. These could be linked to genetic differences in two ways. One is direct. For example, an African race in sub-Saharan Africa has an extremely high occurrence of the Rhesus blood group gene R°, and the sickling group associated with a type of anaemia. The latter obviously has selective behavioural effects. Similarly, the disease known as *phenylketonuria* has a genetic origin, and can cause mental retardation if not identified in infancy. Indirectly, possession of genetically determined characteristics, especially appearance, may control behaviour. Whites and coloureds in South Africa, to take an extreme case, behave differently because they look different. The behaviour is not determined genetically, but the appearance is.

Are there psychological differences between races?
The question arises: have there in fact been observed, psychological differences between races? The answer is certainly yes. Some concern sensori-motor abilities, others perceptual

tendencies. But the greatest controversy has been over intellectual functions, and this will illustrate the general issues. (However, *results* cannot be transferred from, say, the Negro-white question to another pair of groups. The logical points may remain the same, but empirical data cannot be recycled *ad hoc*.)

The data show clearly that there is a considerable difference between the measured IQs of white Americans and Negro Americans. Shuey (1966) exhaustively surveyed some hundreds of studies comparing measured IQs of white and Negro American children, using altogether eighty-one different tests (see page 10 for a discussion of the universality of these tests). They generally found, with a remarkably small variance, that the white children scored fifteen points, or one standard deviation (Fig. 2.1) higher than the coloured. There is little doubt as to the consistency of these studies, and few group differences have proved to be so robust in terms of test–retest reliability. The question is not as to the fact, but as to what it means.

Shuey herself, and others, notably Eysenck and Jensen, believe that they have data which make it a reasonable hypothesis that there is a strong genetic component to the race difference. The reasons advanced (Shuey, 1966; Jensen, 1969; Eysenck, 1971) are manifold. Some of the principal ones are these. Shuey found that IQ differences were greatest on so-called environmentally-free (abstract) test items, and greater for non-verbal than for verbal items. There was, too, a tendency for hybrid groups to score higher than purer Negro groups. Further, the scores of the Negroes were relatively invariant, even across different geographical and school locations.

Jensen and Eysenck also point to the failure of compensatory programmes of education in bringing Negro children up to the level of whites. In particular Jensen contended that the cultural enrichment 'Headstart' programme had failed. Another, the 'Project Learn Well' in San Francisco, was an all-out attempt to improve the scholastic achievement of disadvantaged children (mostly Negroes) by having so small a pupil–teacher ratio as to allow private tutoring of each child. When the progress of these children was compared with state-wide norms, it was found that they had actually fallen behind (cited by Eysenck, 1971).

One very carefully chosen sample of white and black men was studied in order to see whether equating them on a large range of variables would eliminate the observed differences. It has been contended that blacks studied are not properly matched with the white group on socioeconomic variables. Thus the groups were matched on age, education, occupation of parents, income of parents, geographical area of childhood home, army rank, number of years in the service, marital status, urban or rural background, personality, and attitudes to test-taking. But once again differences of nearly one standard deviation were found (cited by Shuey, 1966).

All these facts, it can be argued, point to a genetic component. Moreover Jensen has maintained that rather than attempt to compensate for such differences, education for Negro children should concentrate on what they do best: on, for example, associative rather than conceptual learning. This, of course, is a considerably more contentious suggestion. Neither the practice nor the principles of intellectual assessment nor the role of the intellect in education are understood at more than a rudimentary level. Therefore, to use data of the kind cited by Shuey as evidence in the design of educational courses is, to say the least, hazardous.

Challenges to the nativist theory

The nativist, genetic component account has been severely challenged, with much greater passion than scholarly debate usually arouses. Of course there is not just one issue. Three of the most important questions are: is there a definite, replicable difference between whites and Negroes? If so, is it likely to be environmentally unalterable, i.e. substantially hereditary? If this is so, should the two groups receive different treatment, e.g. in education?

Some of the objections to the hereditary argument are of a logical nature. Here we meet the elderly canard that one cannot measure intelligence because one does not know what it is.

91

Even a knowledgeable author such as Deutsch (1969) blames Jensen for failing to let his readers know that 'g' represents only one theory of intelligence. The answer to this is that we are not interested in the *word* intelligence; we are trying to find tests which assess intellectual skills that are highly regarded, and efficacious, in our culture. 'IQ' or 'intelligence' in this context serve merely as convenient labels.

Another logical objection is that it is impossible to measure the quantitative component that heredity contributes to an attribute. Hebb (1949) argued that to do so is like asking for the amount width contributes to the area of a field or rectangle. But (see Chapter 12) this objection applies only to individuals, not groups.

A methodological objection concerns the purity of the race: that whites and Negroes overlap so much as to make the distinction meaningless. This is irrelevant, since there manifestly are two groups, hybrid as Jensen and Shuey agree them to be.

A different group of objections can be called illogical or emotional. One of us (RK) has heard Professor Eysenck publicly accused of being a conspirator to put racism on a scientific basis. Some, more kindly, regard the nativists as helpless pawns in the hands of reactionary forces of the right, which compel their racist view. As far as we are aware, such objections lack empirical support. Less pleasant arguments include attacks on scientists' personalities, and techniques of suggesting guilt by association.

More serious arguments include these. It has been suggested, plausibly, that Negroes are alienated by white testers; and that they are less well motivated than whites. The evidence is against both these. Shuey compared the results of nineteen studies in which Negro children had been tested by a Negro, with comparable results where a white tester had been used. There was no difference. Tyler (1965) reported a whole series of studies in which increase of motivation by various incentives had had no effect on measured IQ. This was in spite of the fact that Boyd (1952) found Negroes to have a higher level of aspiration than whites.

Tyler does, however, cite data showing that Southern Negroes are inferior to Northern Negroes on measured IQ; and, more conclusively, that Negroes migrating from South to North gain an increment in IQ, which is clear evidence for an environmental component, but there is no guarantee, of course, that such groups are genetically equivalent.

Environmentalists, in the light of such data, have turned to other strategies. Light and Smith (1969), for example, attack Jensen's statistical model on the grounds that it underestimates the variance attributable to the *interaction* of heredity and environment. Other critics assert that Jensen has oversimplified the concept of environment. Another sophisticated objection (Hirsch, 1968) is that the results apply only to the particular populations and environments of each separate study. While logically true, this applies to all scientific observations. Anastasi (1958) and many others have argued cogently that, in discussing the nature–nurture problem the question *how much* each contributes is much less valuable than the question of how they interact.

The weight of evidence, therefore, can be interpreted to suggest that Negroes in the USA score less well on measured IQ, and that the reasons for this include a genetic component. For some discussion of what this might mean, see Chapter 16. What will not do is to deny the evidence. It will be recalled that when Galileo Galilei wanted to show his colleagues the moons of Jupiter, they refused to look through his telescope. Galileo was forced to recant his theory that the earth moved around the sun; but is said, perhaps apocryphally, to have exclaimed on his deathbed *'Eppur si muove!'* ('But it does move!'). Galilean astronomy has been superseded, and so no doubt will be contemporary psychology. The fact that scientific theories are subject to non-scientific influence should not lead us to impose controls on empirical investigation, since only thus can theories be tested.

14
The development of individuality

Although the greatest controversy has centred around intelligence, it is plausible to suppose that there are genetic factors at work in other aspects of individual differences. Indeed we have seen that the long-lived theory of humours implied exactly this. The most popular line of investigation, however, as far as personality factors are concerned, has been to try to establish some physiological basis, or at least correlates, of individual variation, rather than work at partitioning variance as with intellectual functions.

Injury and trauma
There are some cases of severe abnormality that can be seen to have a genetic basis. For example, mongolism is associated with a particular chromosome in triplicate rather than the usual duplicate, giving a total of forty-seven instead of the normal forty-six. Mongolism has nothing to do with the Mongolian people: it is named after a superficial facial resemblance to Asiatic races (the name Down's syndrome is often used now, see F2). It is characterized by a generally restricted development, so that mongols never reach the stage of functioning as fully developed, adult members of society. Similarly, crippling handicaps may occur through traumata (injuries or shocks, mental or physical) during pregnancy or

shortly after birth. Interruption of the oxygen supply to the newly born child may result in brain injury, for example, and thus in mental deficiency. A trauma during pregnancy would result in a condition that was *innate* but not hereditary, a confusion often made.

It is difficult to show that such events relate to specific personality traits. This is partly because we as yet know little about the neurological basis of such traits (see A2). It is also true that the brain at birth is far more plastic than in later life, and can compensate for injury to a remarkable degree. In adults, changes in personality can be the result of brain injury. For a time the operation of pre-frontal leucotomy was frequently used to relieve severe depression. This involves severing the connection between parts of the frontal lobes and the remainder of the brain. Relief of depression could be accompanied by deterioration in personality, the individual becoming less reflective, less able to plan ahead. Similar effects may be due to chemical agents, for example in acute alcoholism. But here it is less easy to distinguish the effects of actual deterioration of the brain from those of physiological and psychological addiction.

Changes in personality may be brought about by malfunctioning of the endocrine system. The endocrine glands secrete substances – hormones – which regulate many aspects of physiological operation. Thus the thyroid gland controls the rate at which the body uses oxygen, the rate at which the engine works, so to speak. Extreme underactivity results in cretinism (characterized by feeblemindedness and certain physiological symptoms). Mild overactivity results in corresponding physical overactivity (but not in genius!).

Physical handicap

Physical handicap, *not* accompanied by brain injury, might be expected to have profound effects on personality (see F2), but no one has as yet discovered any systematic relationship. Unless the handicap is so severe as to prevent all normal interaction with other people from a very early age – and such a case might well hardly survive at all – it seems that, in effect, any type or degree of handicap can be accompanied by any sort of personality development. Many individual cases of the overcoming of handicaps are famous: for example Helen Keller, left blind and deaf from illness in early childhood. A lesser known case is that of John Merrick, described in a book by Ashley Montague called *The Elephant Man: A Study in Human Dignity* (1972). He was so called from a frightful deformity which destroyed any hope of a normal life. Merrick spent years as a circus freak or as the object of ridicule and assault in the streets of callous nineteenth-century London. Yet, rescued from this state, his personality appeared full of kindness and happiness, quite free from the bitterness or malice that might have seemed natural. One can only hope that the thalidomide children of our own time will find similar resources within themselves.

Constitutional factors

There is some evidence to suggest that personality varies with *constitutional* factors. W. H. Sheldon has produced a system of measurement, which has become rather well known, for what are considered to be three basic dimensions of physique, derived from basic physiological components. Any individual can be assessed on each of these (on a 7-point scale); and these scores are held to correlate with those on three varieties of temperament. The system can be summarized as follows:

PHYSIQUE	TEMPERAMENT
Endomorphy – predominance of soft roundness; relative overdevelopment of digestive viscera.	*Visceratonia* – tendency towards relaxation, love of physical comfort, pleasure in eating, sociability.
Mesomorphy – predominance of bone, muscle, and connective tissue; hard, heavy rectangular physique.	*Somatotonia* – tendency towards assertiveness, energetic activity, love of power and risk, physical courage.
Ectomorphy – predominance of linearity and fragility;	*Cerebrotonia* – tendency towards restraint, introversion,

relative to his mass, the
ectomorph has greatest
sensory exposure and largest
brain and nervous system.

love of privacy and solitude,
inhibition.

The validity of this system is not beyond dispute; but even if it were, it is not very easy to see what practical use it is. Little can be done by way of prediction, and one cannot explain physical courage by stating that the individual is a mesomorph – the relationship is not a causal one. Nor, therefore, could behaviour be controlled by altering the body type. However, the system has provided the basis for a science fiction novel, *Doppelgangers*, by Gerald Heard.

Eysenck's theory of personality

A much more far-reaching theory is that of H. J. Eysenck. The theory brings together several lines of research, by Eysenck himself and by others. One line stems from the Russian physiologist, Ivan Pavlov. Pavlov's famous experiments on what is now called classical conditioning (A3), in which a neutral stimulus such as a bell was paired with a stimulus that naturally evoked a response, such as food and salivation respectively, were designed not to elicit the rather obvious fact that eventually the animal will salivate to the bell: they were intended to investigate the working of the nervous system. One of Pavlov's conclusions was that whenever stimuli are paired in this way, a 'connection-forming process', called excitation, occurs in the cortex. Excitation, however, is always accompanied by inhibition, a fatigue-like process that works against the passage of neural impulses. Furthermore, due to innate differences in the cortex, the balance of excitation and inhibition varied between individuals. Some dogs formed conditioned responses rapidly, and retained them well; others the opposite. Pavlov's dogs also showed varied reactions to other experimental situations, so much so that he was able to classify them into different 'personality types'. These types turned out to be rather similar to the human types of the theory of humours.

Another source of Eysenck's theory was the personality typology of C. G. Jung. Jung, originally like Adler a follower of Freud, developed from his psychiatric and other observations an account of personality in which there is always a kind of balance of opposites. Whatever aspects are overt or apparent on the surface, their opposites or counterparts are present unconsciously. One of these pairs is extraversion-introversion. From the results of his factor-analytic studies, Eysenck transformed this into a dimension of personality. On the basis of this Eysenck believes he can predict behaviour over a wide range of individual and social variables (see D1, D3).

Development through experience
In contrast to these approaches are theories that emphasize individual development through particular patterns of experience.

Freud, although he thought that it would eventually be possible to find a physiological basis for mental events, concentrated in fact on the psychological level. For Freud, the individual, developed personality may be said to be the result of patterns of emotional reactions in early childhood. In those years are determined the relative roles of conscious and unconscious factors. As is well known, Freud described a series of psychosexual stages of development through which every child is said to pass. He considered that if the progress was not satisfactory, later behaviour could be dominated by a group of characteristics associated with a particular stage: for example, the obstinate and miserly 'anal type', etc. The evidence for these personality syndromes is at best highly equivocal. However, perhaps a greater difficulty is that psychoanalytic theory does not tell us *what* variables in the environment will tend to bring about particular patterns of development.

Presumably there must be factors, particularly in the family, which will favour certain personalities. One attempt to investigate this was that of Adorno and others (1949) who described the *authoritarian* personality, supposedly the result of a rigid, hierarchical family system with little room for the free expression of emotion between parents and children. Unfortunately this attractive and plausible concept has not, on the whole, been supported by subsequent research. In somewhat similar vein Harvey, Hunt, and Schroder (1961) developed what was known as conceptual systems theory. The general idea was that in an environment allowing maximum room for exploration (of things, ideas, feelings) and maximum feedback of information, an individual – a child – will develop a high level of organization of concepts, resulting in ability to think abstractly, to be creative and adaptable to new situations (compare *The Children on the Hill*, Chapter 16).

Cultural variation

Evidence is hard to come by, due partly to the fact that one cannot deliberately manipulate child-rearing to any great extent. Cross-cultural studies may help (see C5). For example, Dawson (1963, 1967) examined Witkin's concept of *field dependence*. Roughly, this refers to the extent to which judgments, especially perceptual judgments, are made under the influence of the environment. This can be measured in several ways, one of the simplest being based on ability to pick out figures 'embedded' in a more complex drawing. Dawson took such tests to two West African communities, the Temne and the Mende. He found as he had predicted, that field dependence in men correlated with their reports of the strictness of their mothers when bringing them up. Berry (1966) likewise found that Eskimo children were relatively field independent. They grow up in an environment in which independence, freedom, and the cultivation of skills are encouraged, and punishment is rarely used.

Such reports are suggestive rather than conclusive, due to the complexities of cross-cultural work. Historical data also at least suggest, however, that some cultures encourage a greater degree of individuality than others (see D2). In our favourite example of classical Greece it is clear that great weight was put upon individual excellence. In Athens, certain offices of state were filled by lot, any citizen being equally eligible. It is also clear that exceptional heights were attained in many fields – philosophy, science, the arts, statesmanship. It would be rash

99

though to claim that one caused the other: see Kitto (1953) for an illuminating discussion.

Self-actualization

Of late, a good deal of attention has been paid to the development of individuality in the sense of a full or balanced personality, fulfilment of potential, and the like. Among the sources of this interest, as we have noted, were Allport and Carl Rogers. Jung, too, wrote much of *individuation*: the integration of the conscious and unconscious aspects of the personality. Perhaps the leading figure, however, has been Abraham Maslow. Maslow argued that psychologists had over-emphasized negative aspects of human motivation, such as anxiety reduction, and 'lower' needs such as hunger. They ought to pay attention to needs for joy, aesthetic experience, self-fulfilment. Maslow accepted the importance of basic needs, which however he extended to include affection, security, self-esteem. But he stressed the importance of 'meta needs', whose fulfilment accompanies what he termed *self-actualization*. Maslow considered that this level of development was achieved by very few. Some of these rare individuals Maslow sought out and studied. He concluded they had many characteristics in common: few, but profound, emotional relationships; strong need for privacy and detachment; independence; creativity and sense of humour. Above all, perhaps, openness to what he calls 'peak experiences': high intensity experiences of an aesthetic, spiritual, or emotional kind.

One of the great problems with all this is that, so far, it has proved extremely difficult to investigate objectively. It is really by no means clear how self-actualization is to be assessed, or what variables are supposed to contribute to it. However it is certainly true that psychology has not yet really attempted to deal with such clearly important aspects of human variability; and for directing attention to them Maslow deserves credit.

15
Sex differences

It is said that Dr Samuel Johnson was once asked which is more intelligent, man or woman. He replied, 'Which man, which woman?'

Differences between groups

If true, the doctor was both right and wrong in his answer. Right, because the two groups overlap in terms of measured intelligence. Wrong, because it is legitimate to consider differences between the *means* of the two groups as indicative of sex differences in intelligence. In order to do so, we must employ statistical reasoning. It is an old cry that 'you can prove anything with statistics', and in some contexts such as advertising and politics they are certainly open to abuse. Statistical inference, however, is at the heart of scientific method. This is more apparent in psychology due to the greater variability of the subject-matter. In dealing with sex differences we have to all intents two groups only (we can disregard cases of physiological bisexuality, and persons who have undergone sex-change operations, as these are very few in number and there is little data on them). The principles of group comparison, however, are the same however many the groups. When differences are recorded, these are rarely if ever based on observations of all possible members of the groups – all men and all women. Only a sample can be observed. A difference is generally said to be statistically significant if there is at least a 95 per cent chance of a difference of this size being present in the parent population (see A8).

This should cause psychologists to pay attention to three matters, though often enough one or more is neglected. One is the appropriateness of the procedures used to calculate significance. This is a complex technical matter into which we shall not enter. The second is the representativeness of the sample actually studied. It is well known that very many psychological studies are done on compulsorily 'volunteered' students. These may or may not be appropriate for more general conclusions. The third point is that it is necessary to have, at least, several items of statistical information. One is the mean or arithmetic average; another is the range or total dispersion of scores; another is the form of the distribution. Even these basic conditions are not always met.

Differences between the sexes

The study of sex differences has yielded a great deal of data, partly for the reasons just stated of variable worth. Apart from anecdote, there is a wealth of descriptive studies by psychologists, sociologists, and anthropologists. Explanations of the data are, as so often, more difficult to obtain.

There has been, in the study of sex differences, an ideological component at least since the rise of feminism at the turn of the century. Thus many of the studies have been devoted to testing traditional lore about the different abilities, temperaments, and personalities of the two groups. Of 300 studies surveyed by Miles (1935) many were allegedly 'motivated by the desire to demonstrate that females were not inherently inferior to males' (Tyler, 1956). The general conclusion from these studies was that the feminists' claims were vindicated. Differences in mental abilities were small and attributable to environmental factors. There was considerable overlap in the scores of the two sexes. At the same time, the sexes were differentiated by different *patterns* of abilities.

During the 1930s the research emphasis changed from

intellectual to orectic (emotional and motivational) attributes, and the object was rather to achieve a better understanding of the differences. Differences rather naturally appeared in the areas of interests, values, attitudes, emotional needs, and the like. The recognition of these differences was followed by the establishment of a standardized test of Masculinity–Femininity, as it is conceived in our culture. In the 1960s and 70s, Women's Lib. has brought many of the issues to the fore again. Some of these are concerned with rights, others with facts. We shall concentrate on the latter, but the two interact in a complex way.

Learning sex-roles

It is one of the most obvious things in the world that sex is inherited; children do not, it would seem, need to be taught which sex they are. This is partly true, and partly false. Physiology is inherited, but it is not inevitably accompanied by sex-typed patterns of behaviour.

Probably the most famous studies here have been those of the anthropologist, Margaret Mead, reported in *Sex and Temperament in Three Primitive Societies* (1939) and other books. The three primitive societies were all tribes in New Guinea, and they were sharply differentiated by the pattern of male and female personality which they displayed, according to Mead. Among the *Arapesh* both men and women displayed emotional characteristics which in Western society would be labelled distinctly feminine. Both sexes were trained to be cooperative, unaggressive, gentle, non-competitive, and responsive to the needs of others. The *Mundugumor* presented a sharply contrasting picture. In that society, both men and women were violent, aggressive, ruthless and competitive, taking great delight in action and in fighting. But even more remarkable, from our viewpoint, was the behaviour of the *Tchambuli*, among whom there appeared to be a reversal of the sex attitudes present in our culture. It was the women who had the position of power, since they were responsible for fishing and for the manufacture of mosquito bags, which provided the chief articles of trade for the tribe. The men, on the other hand, engaged predominantly in artistic and other non-utilitarian pursuits, most being skilled

103

in dancing, carving, painting or other arts. With regard to personality, *Tchambuli* women were described as impersonal, practical, and efficient, while the men were graceful, artistic, emotionally subservient, timid, and sensitive to the opinions of others.

This sort of approach, to which the title 'modal personality' has been attached, would probably be now regarded by anthropologists as rather simple-minded. Nevertheless, it does seem fairly well established that most of the orectic characteristics of femininity and masculinity are learned. This is supported by sociological and psychological studies. However the mechanisms involved appear to be extremely complex, and various terms are in circulation. Probably the broadest is socialization, referring to all the processes by which an individual takes on the psychological characteristics of members of his culture. Of this, sex-role typing is one aspect. From the child's point of view, a number of processes are involved. One is receiving *instruction*, deliberate or incidental – from family, peer groups, mass media, school (see C4). Another is *imitation*. It is well established that this depends upon very many factors, including the status of persons imitated, family structure, rewards attached to imitative behaviour (see B1). A third is *identification*, the relation of which to imitation is not entirely clear. However, both seem to play a part in sex-role typing. Of the many empirical studies, a number have concentrated on the child's perception of his parents. Mussen, for example, found that highly masculine boys perceived their father as more nurturant than less masculine boys. Kagan and Moss found that girls scoring highly on need for achievement and aggression (see D2), tend to perceive their mothers as cold and hostile and their fathers as warm and nurturant. The exact relationship between these variables is not yet clear. One hypothesis is that children identify with a person who is either nurturant *or* aggressive. (The concept of identification with the aggressor derives from Freud.)

Aptitudes and abilities
More straightforward, though still sometimes puzzling, are the

sex differences in certain aptitudes. Some of these are predictable from sex-role typing. For instance, even in infancy boys are stronger, faster, and better at locomotion than girls (Gesell *et al.*, 1940). Girls, however, are superior at manual dexterity. Differences not completely predictable from common sense are found in perception. Girls excel in the perception of detail, as do adult women (Andrew *et al.*, 1946). However, spatial orientation is more accurately perceived by men, who are also more field independent (Witkin *et al.*, 1954). The top role is similarly shared in language use. Women are superior in word fluency, but not in verbal comprehension (Herberg and Lepkin, 1954).

Many of the sex differences between boys and girls are neutralized by the time of adulthood. This is largely because girls mature earlier than boys, in many respects. They reach physical maturity sooner, and throughout childhood are further advanced towards their adult status. The differences, taken age for age, disappear when both sexes are adult. Anastasi (1958) reports that the developmental superiority of girls can only be established with reference to physical attributes. It has not been found that girls have an advantage in mental attributes such as intelligence over boys of the same age.

Interests and attitudes
In some areas, psychologists have done studies which provide precise data on well-known differences (in our culture). Thus there is evidence for consistent differences in interests and attitudes. Boys play more aggressive games than girls do. In reading and in the mass media, boys prefer adventure stories, girls romances. The vocational intentions of high school students (USA) show that boys desire jobs offering power and profit, while girls place higher value on social service. Numerous studies, such as Watson (1948), confirm the male idea that there are differences in conversation. Internationally, there is a consistent pattern: men talk most about money, business affairs, and sport; women talk most frequently about other women and clothes. It is unknown, of course, how this has been affected by the Women's Liberation Movement. Anastasi (1958)

summarizes a wealth of data with the verdict that sex differences in interests, preferences, attitudes, and values reveal the greater social orientation of females. This possibly has two components, an interest in people, and an altruistic element. Women early show greater interest in people, men in things. However, a study of 3000 college students by Johnson and Terman did not find that women behaved more socially, although they desired more strongly to be social.

Achievement

As is well known, women are exceeded by men in achievements in adulthood. Ellis (1904), studying 1030 British persons of genius, counted only fifty-five women. More surprising is a very consistent finding that girls exceed boys at school achievement tasks – in examinations, in rate of progress, in memory, and in many other factors. That these results are due to multiple causes is clear. It should also be noted that many of the differences are due to lack of opportunity. For instance, women commit fewer crimes than men, as well as achieving less; and this is partly due to lack of opportunity. In general, whatever the causes, it may be that men are more variable than women: there are more male mental deficients, as well as more geniuses. Men are more at risk from all sorts of causes throughout life.

However much sex-role behaviour is learned, though, there must be some that remains innate. Principally, only women can bear and succour children: they must play a different role in a family to a man. The current fashion is to diminish the differences as far as possible. It is one thing to establish equality of opportunity: but it is also possible to argue that an arrangement in which men and women have relatively clearly defined, distinct roles can be at least as successful as one where they are blurred or nonexistent. We do not wish to argue for one or the other: merely to point out that fashion is not all.

16
Culture
and individuality

In view of the unresolved nature–nurture problems, it is quite
difficult to make any really certain statements about the effects
of culture, which is only a part, though for humans probably
the most important part, of the environment. It is true that in
both nature and nurture there are some cases of specific defici-
encies having specific effects. For example cretinism is the
direct result of thyroid deficiency, and haemophilia is due to a
particular genetic structure. But in culture even such limited
findings are absent. By 'culture' we may mean, broadly, the
environment insofar as this is a human product. There are no
simple one-to-one effects here. But science cannot wait on
perfect data, and we must make shift to infer what we can.

Among the questions we should like to be able to answer are
these. To what extent can we attribute human variance to
cultural factors? Are cultural differences in some sense fundamental – do manners really make the man? Do some cultures
produce a greater degree of variability than others? Do some
lead to particular *sorts* of variation?

Conflict of cultures
On the face of it, there are clear differences between cultures;
so much so that at times one has the greatest difficulty in
understanding the other. An example is the collapse of the

formal, ritualistic Aztec civilization before a handful of ruthless Spanish adventurers. Throughout history cases abound of one group destroying, as far as lay in its power, the culture and the very lives of another. Upon the European discovery of the Pacific, debate raged as to whether the indigenous populations were members of the human race or merely animals. In the event, many were decimated and some, such as the Tasmanians, utterly destroyed. Attitudes as strange, if less drastic, are to be noted within our own culture. Nineteenth-century scholars puzzled why England should not have produced a folk music, while in fact a tradition still flourished hardly surpassed in length and richness. Indeed it may be suggested (D1) that the civilized requires the barbaric almost in order to exist.

Psychological differences between cultures

However this may be, there is some evidence of psychological variation between cultures. Gregory (1966), for example, reports experiments showing that Zulus are less susceptible to the Müller-Lyer (arrowheads) illusion than are Europeans – surprisingly, since many similar illusions are known to affect animals which suggests that they do not have a cultural origin. There is a long and confused dispute as to whether different cultures 'think' differently. One of the most obvious starting-points is that they obviously speak differently. Language is clearly closely connected with thought (see A7), and one theory, propounded by the nineteenth-century philologist, Max Müller, and championed by Benjamin Lee Whorf, is that the structure of the language controls the way we structure the world. Indeed it has been argued forcibly, if vaguely, by Basil Bernstein that even within the same language, different 'codes' are available to children from different social classes, and that this affects the way they think. The alternative view is that language is merely a means of expression: the thought is the same, though the label is different. Perhaps the prevailing opinion is that the whole thing is far more complex than either simple view. Bruner, for example (see C2), sees language as one form (though the most subtle and powerful) of one of three *modes* of representing the environment or thinking. This view is at

108

least not inconsistent with those of many other leading theorists such as Piaget, Freud, Vygotsky, Neisser (see Radford and Burton, 1974).

Another prevailing argument has been over the concept of 'primitive' societies, and the 'primitive' way in which they have been supposed to think (see C4). Perhaps the most famous exponent of this was the French sociologist Lucien Levy-Bruhl (e.g. *How Natives Think*, 1910). Levy-Bruhl used the term 'pre-logical', suggesting that the thinking of non-literate peoples more-or-less corresponded to an earlier stage of development of the race, and indeed to that of children. This view, while not inconsistent with much nineteenth-century anthropology, has been under fairly continuous attack ever since. For example, Robin Horton has argued (e.g. 1967) that it is a mistake to imagine, in a rather simple way, that Western people think 'scientifically' as opposed to others, such as Africans, who think 'magically'. Both are engaged in trying to understand their world by developing explanatory theories. Both first tackle events by means of common sense and practical experience; if these fail, they go on to a higher order of explanation. This is plausible to an extent, and it is quite likely that, for example, a Western housewife's faith in the virtues of disinfectant is no more 'scientific' than belief in a rabbit's foot. (We are not aware of any experimental research on such beliefs.) The obvious difference is that disinfectant can be shown to work by actually destroying germs; the rabbit's foot cannot. But to follow this up would lead us too far afield.

Intelligence and culture
Psychologists have tended to concentrate on more testable areas, especially intelligence. P. E. Vernon (1969) has given us a comprehensive review of this work. He presents evidence, for example, for the effects of a whole range of environmental handicaps:

1 physiological and nutritional deficit
2 perceptual deprivation in pre-school years
3 repression of independence and constructive play

4 family insecurity and lack of playfulness
5 female dominance (this may favour verbal as compared to spatial abilities)
6 defective education
7 linguistic handicaps
8 adult roles and adolescent aspirations (in minority cultures, children may be affected by gradual realization of their depressed status, lack of opportunities, etc.).

The first thing to note is that what these handicaps affect is *Intelligence C* (p. 65): the sample taken by tests or other measures. But these measures derive from a different culture – in which, for example, fathers may be dominant. The next thing is that, apart from physiological handicaps (such as deafness, for example) it is very hard to see just what constitutes a deficit. Was Shakespeare's education deficient? Ben Jonson said he had small Latin and less Greek, and he certainly had no 'O' levels or 'A' levels. Vernon concludes: '. . . it seems reasonable to regard the Puritan ethic of the western middle class as producing the greatest development of intelligence, in contrast both to western lower class and to the "less civilised" cultures.'

Such a conclusion is reasonable only if we are very clear that 'intelligence' means 'scores on Western middle class tests'. To apply such tests elsewhere may have two uses. One is for prediction. Simply as a matter of fact, performance on tests often correlates well with success in education or work, particularly if these are themselves Western-oriented. In itself, this can be a useful fact. The second use is for research. Again it is, in itself, important to know how different groups compare on standardized instruments, just as it is to record height and weight.

Problems of cross-cultural research
However, even this very limited purpose is beset by problems. Warburton (1951), for example, describes the testing of Ghurka recruits. They showed no wish to hurry on tests, no competi-

tiveness – attitudes which are natural to us at least from primary school onwards. In other words, the 'test' was not, for the Ghurkas, a test as we understand it. (Warburton remarks that because the apparatus was made of wood the psychologist was known as the wood officer.) Frijda and Jahoda (1966) discuss in detail the extreme problems of making fair comparisons. For example, it is often very hard to get accurate data about, say, ages: but even if this is overcome, the whole developmental sequence may be different, so that chronological equivalence may mean little or nothing. In an interesting study of the Kpelle people of Liberia (see C4), Michael Cole and others (1971) found that the concept of being clever simply was not applied to tasks such as building a house or repairing a car: 'cleverness' was shown in social relations – for example in how well parents understood the principles of bringing up children.

Thus to speak of handicaps may itself be misleading. This view is urged, among others, by Labov (e.g. 1970), particularly with reference to different racial groups in the United States. It is not, he argues, a matter of groups being potentially equal, but sometimes handicapped by poor schooling, poor environment, etc. Rather, potential, and even actual, achievement, cannot be reliably inferred from performance. Those who do poorly on tests may show in different situations equally complex skills. This sort of argument would help to account for the relative lack of success of 'Headstart' programmes.

Experiment

It also leads to a more detailed kind of experimental anthropological research designed to tease out the variables in an environment that lead to different styles of cognitive development. For example Vernon found that a particular task of fitting triangular pieces together to make a number of shapes was especially difficult for Ugandan children. He suggested that this might be because most African babies are bound to, and carried on, their mother's backs for the first year or two of life. Thus not only is their field of vision restricted – largely to one rounded object – but they get very little experience of handling things. Glick (1968), another of the Harvard school to which

111

Cole belongs, asked some of his Kpelle subjects to sort various objects. Whereas a Westerner might put an orange together with an apple because both are fruit, the typical Kpelle response was to put it with a knife, since the knife cuts the orange. Thus, Glick argues, it is practical experience that forms the basis of categorizing. Another example: Price-Williams (1969) tried out some of Piaget's well-known 'conservation' tasks with Mexican children (see C2). The issue is whether children realize that, given a quantity of any material, the amount remains the same despite changes in shape. Some of the subjects were the children of potters, used to handling clay. These were better at conservation. As Price-Williams argues, it is not just a case of playing with clay, but of specific skills required to make cups or what not.

Family style

It might be expected that individual differences would come about through particular variations in family upbringing even within a culture. There are some suggestions that this is so. For example Albert (1971) examined the life histories of a large number of persons reckoned as 'eminent' or 'historical geniuses'. He found that as compared to the average college population, three times as many had lost at least one parent by the age of ten. Such an observation raises far more questions than it answers. First there could be all sorts of circumstances, including genetic ones, that make the two populations not comparable. Setting that aside, there are questions about the possible role of parent substitutes – uncles, tutors, etc; about whether parental loss makes children more dependent or independent; etc. In another fascinatingly suggestive study Carlsmith (1964) examined the effect of the absence of fathers from their families due to the Second World War. This was a rather neat natural experiment manipulating the variable of 'father absence'. Carlsmith found that the sons of fathers who had been away for long periods were relatively better in verbal skills than in mathematics, whereas those whose fathers had remained at home showed the opposite. In general, boys normally do better at mathematical, and girls on verbal tests,

112

and it is plausible to suppose that this has something to do with sex-role identification. But why should this be so, and how does it work? Numerous other studies available similarly raise further questions. The reader may care to compare such work with an account of a remarkable family, *The Children on the Hill* by Michael Deakin (1973). A pair of most unusual parents is described as deliberately bringing up their children, clearly highly gifted, not without discipline but with none of the usual restraints upon curiosity and exploration that ordinary family life entails. Whether the result will be a group of adult geniuses remains to be seen.

We have discussed mainly cognitive differences; see also *Sex differences* (Chapter 15). One conclusion that stands out amid the jungle of variables is the range of human adaptability. It is a commonplace that we are the only species to inhabit all parts of the surface of the earth. In the 1830s it was thought that the human frame would never stand up to the velocity of steam trains; now, men seem unharmed by space flight.

Indigenous man as creator

Adaptability is accompanied by heterogeneity. And it can be argued that from these two factors come what we like to think of as our greatest achievements. Flinders Petrie, the great archaeologist, hypothesized that new civilizations arise always from the mixing of two diverse peoples. If this is so it is unfortunate that we are engaged in destroying with the utmost speed every culture in the world but one. George Appell of Brandeis University is among the rather few champions of indigenous man, not as 'primitive', but as creator, inventor, discoverer. He shows how in every part of the world man has evolved, over thousands of years, a productive relationship with nature. Each culture has acquired a vast stock of knowledge of natural products, and in so doing maintained a vital pool of variability. To cite but one example, in Borneo each separate village has traditionally maintained ten to twenty varieties of dry-cultivation rice, selected for taste and productivity in the particular environment. Current government policy is to replace all these with universal wet-rice agriculture, and relocate whole populations from hill areas to places more suitable for irrigation. Nearer home we can point to the loss of local variation in everything from cheese to clothes, dialect to building materials. The situation is unprecedented, and the consequences unknown.

17
Gordon W. Allport

Gordon Willard Allport was born on 22 November 1897, in Indiana, USA. His father was a medical doctor. His mother was of Scottish and German descent. The upbringing of the family – Gordon was the youngest of four sons – was humanitarian-religious.

From 1903 to 1915 Gordon followed his pre-college education, graduating from High School second out of one hundred. He went to Harvard, where his elder brother, Floyd, was already a postgraduate in psychology, and read economics and philosophy, in a double major, for four years, whereupon he received his BA degree. After graduation Gordon Allport taught English and sociology for one year at Robert College, Istanbul, Turkey. He then returned to Harvard and obtained in 1921 his MA and in 1922 his PhD, both in psychology. Subsequently, with the aid of a travelling scholarship, he spent two years in Europe. He attended courses at the Universities of Berlin and Hamburg. The next academic year, 1923–4, he studied at the University of Cambridge, England. He then returned to Harvard as an instructor, and in 1925 married a clinical psychologist. They had a son who became a paediatrician. Gordon Allport was pleased to see himself sandwiched between two physicians, father and son.

Allport taught for four years at Dartmouth College and in

September 1930 rejoined the staff of Harvard. He was instrumental in the foundation, in 1946, of the Department of Social Relations, in which he served for twenty-one years, until his death in 1967.

Allport formed his main ideas early in his career and in essence held to them thereafter. He had two main concerns: the problem of personality, and social problems. He had an active concern for helping people – as an undergraduate he worked in several social services – and divided his time between social ethics and social problems, and personality.

In 1920 Allport met Freud in Vienna. During the meeting Allport told the true story of a phobic boy of four years of age whom he had recently encountered. When Allport finished the story, Freud said kindly: 'And was that little boy you?' Allport was horrified by Freud's apparent assumption that his motives were not manifest, and the consequent imputation of neurosis. The incident started, in Allport's words, 'a deep train of thought', and in due course was a strong contributing factor in his elaboration of a psychology of rationality, of normality, of the fully-evolved self.

He began to study deeply the available theories of human nature and personality, and brought to this task an encyclopaedic, eclectic mind. Some ten years after the completion of his studies he published his classic *Personality*. Here he dismissed existing theories as partial, and insisted on the *individuality* of the person, and on traits as the fundamental units of personality. His PhD dissertation had been *An experimental study of the traits of personality*. Allport was apparently the first American psychologist to teach a course on personality. When the book was published it was thought controversial and polemical, but subsequently became a standard text.

In 1931 Allport published *A Study of Values*, an investigation of the individual's central interests. Further publications include his 1948 work on case studies of individuals; *The Nature of Prejudice* (1950); *The Individual and His Religion* (1951). A small, 100-page book published in 1955, *Becoming: Basic Conditions for a Science of Personality*, gives a good summary of his views.

Allport found himself in opposition to much of the prevailing psychology of his day, partly because of his European training. His independent outlook led him to reject behaviourism with its apparent reduction of man to a complicated machine. However, he also held, as against Freud, that man throughout life can develop or 'become'. Psychoanalytic theory, he felt, put too great stress on the determining events of the first three years. Allport asserted: 'Becoming is a fundamental law of life . . . every personality develops continually from infancy unto death, and persists though it changes.' What perseveres is the 'metaphysical self'; what changes is the 'psychological self'. Becoming is the essential psychological feature of man. Personality changes cumulatively and by integration. Man is not a simple but a complex unity, permanently differentiating by maturation and learning. Integration confers unity on the individual's components but there is no wholly unified personality because in life there is no finished becoming. Death is the end of becoming.

Allport, like his contemporary Henry Murray, regarded man as pro-active. Part of what this means is that it is not possible to account for an individual's functioning in any situation by looking only at the external features of that situation, since man has internal processes that control the way he experiences the situation. While this may seem relatively obvious now, it was less so when behaviourism was at the height of its influence (and of course the pendulum may swing again). Another aspect is that behaviour is forward-looking; it is aimed at something, not just pushed along by drives or stimuli. (This would have come as no surprise to McDougall or indeed to Aristotle.) A related concept of Allport's is the functional autonomy of adult motives. For example, a man might set out to do well in business in order to provide for his family; but often his career success itself may then become the real motivation.

The general goal of development, however, is organization and integration. In this process, personality is an open system that is continually interacting with the environment. Allport is very clearly the precursor of such 'humanistic' psychologists as Rogers and Maslow (see D1 and D3). Allport also put great

117

stress on the rational nature of man. The long-range plans, and philosophies of life, that Allport considered controlled much of what we do, are conscious activities. Partly for this reason Allport emphasized the importance of subjective experience and self-reports for understanding a person. For example, he thought projective techniques quite useless for adults: one could get the same information much more simply by asking them directly. In line with this, he developed new techniques of gathering information, for example, from the study of personal documents.

Allport's biographer, Ghougassian, reports that: 'the principle of uniqueness . . . obsessed Allport'. The problems this gives rise to are mentioned elsewhere (see p. 28). In *Pattern and Growth in Personality* (1961), Allport listed eleven methods for studying uniqueness. Perhaps alone among psychologists, he was keen that psychology should learn from literature, where we see depicted traits, characterological self-sufficiency, and the sustained interest in one person at one time. Literature and science in his view (and RK's) should collaborate, thus allowing us to deal with both uniqueness and generality.

18
Interests and values

Interests

To most individual persons, their interests and their values are among the most important of their attributes. Super (1949) has cautioned that there have, from the point of view of measurement, been four major interpretations of the term 'interest', each being connected with a different method of collecting data. The first type of interest he calls *expressed interest*, which he defines as the verbal profession of interest in an object, activity, task, or occupation. In this case the subject is required to say of each item that he either likes, dislikes, or is indifferent to it. The second type is called *manifest interest*; this is synonymous with participation in an activity or occupation. Super also calls this the 'objective manifestation of an interest'.

The third category is called *tested interest*. This is a stricter form of its immediate predecessor. Tested interest refers to interest as measured by objective tests controlled by the experimenter (as opposed to the subject in the previous case). The fourth type is called *inventoried interest*. This is interest as measured by inventories which are composed of lists of activities and occupations. The subject makes a response to each item, as often occurs with *expressed interest*. But inventoried interest measurements have a crucial addition: each response in the inventory is given an experimentally determined weight. The weights corresponding to the answers given by the person completing the inventory are added in order to yield a score which represents, not a single subjective estimate as in the case of expressed interest, but a pattern of interests which research has shown to be stable. The best known example of inventoried interest is the 'Strong Vocational Interest Blank', published by Strong (1927), and this will be our main concern. Since 1927, the Blank has been given to hundreds of thousands of persons in both counselling and research situations, and a large bibliography concerning it has accumulated.

The measurement of interest
Strong selected four hundred items of many kinds – occupations, school subjects, recreational activities, etc. – and employed a large group of subjects to complete the Blank in order that the initial weights might be calculated. Because the test was developed in the setting of applied psychology, the weighting was primarily in terms of professions or occupations. The original respondents marked each item 'Like', 'Dislike', or 'Indifferent'. Scoring keys were then developed by considering each item in turn and, for each, comparing the responses of the subjects in a particular profession with the responses of 'men in general' – i.e. the rest of the respondents. In this way each profession was thus compared on each item. Any response for which the difference in percentage was statistically significant was part of the scoring key for that particular profession. Weights were attached to items according to the size of the difference. In developing the 'Engineer' key, for example, it was found that 47 per cent of men in general as compared with 60 per cent of his engineers marked the item 'Actor' 'Dislike'. This led to the inclusion of the D response on 'Actor' as part of the 'Engineer' scoring key, with one point of credit. To another item, 'Author of technical book', 50 per cent of engineers, but only 31 per cent of others, said 'Like'. This response difference caused the 'Like' response to be given three points of credit for that key.

To the pure differential psychologist, this instrument has assets and faults. An asset is that it has a certain amount of construct validity (see p. 37) built into it. We cannot necessarily say just what it is that differentiates engineers from others, but we can help persons to compare themselves with engineers. The fault is that the measurement scale in use is uncertain. As Tyler (1967) observes, if a respondent scores much *more* than a typical group on their key (say, the average musician scores 100 on the musician key, and a respondent scores 150), it does not mean that he is a sort of super-musician, or likely to be more successful. But it does seem to suggest that the interest is not only stronger but more enduring (Layton, 1960).

A second fault of the Blank is its limitation to vocational interest, and of its categories to occupational groups. In this, perhaps, lies its strength from a practical viewpoint. Certainly the Blank has been shown to have good predictive validity. Strong (1955) was able to confirm that the following predictions had been upheld:

1 Men continuing in occupation X obtain a higher interest score on X than on any other occupation.
2 Men continuing in occupation X obtain a higher interest score in it than do other men entering other occupations.
3 Men continuing in occupation X obtain higher scores in X than do men who change from X to another occupation.
4 Men changing from occupation X to occupation Y score higher on Y prior to the change than on any other occupation, including X.

Apart from this impressive testimony to the value of Strong's Blank, the applied psychologist might also argue that he has devised an instrument for measuring individual differences which are at least among the most important to be measured; for not only are the occupational distinctions basic to our (Western) culture; they are also in a very obvious sense highly important in a person's life: people spend the majority of their waking hours, the majority of their adulthood, engaged in their occupations. And, since the measuring

121

instrument has been worked out and shown to be successful, what more could be asked?

But of course a good deal more could be asked. At the least, we would ask about the correlation of occupational interest to other personality dimensions; and we would ask for the principal dimensions of interest to be examined empirically – that is, not in terms of predetermined categories, but in terms of the variation found in the data. Finally, we would seek some explanation of the data. All these would apply equally to studies of non-vocational interest. Fortunately, there are some studies which bear on these problems.

Cattell and Guilford, for example, have tried to incorporate interest variations into a more inclusive theory of human personality and motivation. There has thus been a considerable amount of correlation research attempting to link interests to other aspects of personality. One of the most striking results was that the correlations between interest tests and the sort of personality inventories developed out of psychiatric thinking have been close to zero. The most consistent correlation was with values. Dukes (1955), reviewing instances of correlations between values and interests, found seven significant correlations.

Much energy has also been expended on trying to identify the basic dimensions of interest by factor analysis and cluster analysis. Neither Guilford nor Cattell have directly relevant data here, as they have subordinated 'interest' to 'motivation'. However, the Strong Blank has been used in factor and cluster analyses. The findings are complex. Not unnaturally, the factors vary according to the method of analysis used, and the naming of the factors is always difficult, as there is no guarantee that the correlations will arrange themselves so that a convenient factor loading comes to mind. However, the results may be summarized thus: A cluster analysis by Thurstone (1932) yielded four factors, which he labelled (1) interest in science; (2) interest in language; (3) interest in people; (4) interest in business. It is amusing (or disquieting) to note that psychologists correlated zero with interest in people.

However, Eysenck (1970) feels that nothing like finality has been reached in the classification of interests, and that indeed the field is somewhat retarded.

Values

As with interests, the study of values has been dominated by a single work. This work, however, was from within psychology, rather than from applied psychology. It is the famous 'Study of Values' (Allport and Vernon, 1931; Allport, Vernon and Lindzey, 1951). *A Study of Values* was inspired by the German philosopher Spranger, who was attempting to devise a typology of men in terms of their value-orientation. He proposed that there were six basic value types, and that every man approaches one or more of these types. He is not asserting necessarily that every man falls into one and only one type; the typology uses 'ideal-types'. The phrase does not mean that the types are pure or good; rather it refers to the fact that life is rarely as neat as the idealized types which we use. Spranger seemed to assert, however, not that there were definitely six types of men, but six types of values.

The six basic value-types, with brief explanations, are as follows:

1 *The theoretical*: primary concern is truth, knowledge, and their organization.
2 *The economic*: primary concern is with the *useful* and the practical.
3 *The aesthetic*: primary concern with form and harmony, at the expense of truth or practicality.
4 *The social*: the highest value is love of people.
5 *The political*: the highest value is *power*.
6 *The religious*: the highest value is *unity*.

A Study of Values is based on this typology. Allport, who was the originator of the test, describes it as a 'somewhat complex test of six common traits'. It is a pencil and paper test. The method used is a forced-choice question-and-answer one; that is, for each question there is a limited number of answers, of which each respondent *must* choose one. In part I of the test, each of the six values is paired an equal number of times with each of the remaining five. A typical question is 'Which of the following branches of study do you expect ultimately will prove more important for mankind? (a) Mathematics, (b) Theology?' Respondents can score an answer 2-1 or 3-0 according to the strength of the preference. In part II each question has four possible answers, and the subject places them in rank order of preference. There are thirty questions in part I and fifteen in part II. When all the forty-five items have been scored, the total preference accorded each of the six values is recorded. The data are, however, only an ordinal scale of measurement; the profile shows the relative importance of the values in a respondent's life. However, the test yields norms. 8369 subjects were asked to complete the questionnaire, and the results were broken down by sex, college, and occupation. Allport (1961) reports that the test–retest reliability is excellent, as is the item-reliability. He also contends that the construct validation is provided by the use of the test in differentiating occupations. Clergymen have high religious and social values, engineers have high theoretical and economic values, and so on.

Allport is very candid about the strengths and weaknesses of the test. He suggests that it helps people to be more self-insightful. Thus it is useful in teaching, counselling, and marriage guidance. As far as the weaknesses are concerned, Allport feels that the values listed by Spranger are idealist in a normative as well as a theoretical sense: that is, Spranger neglects the baser motives of value systems. In particular, sensuality and opportunism are neglected. Such an admittal is a cue for a discussion about the 'basic values'. Predictably, Allport feels that factor analysis could do little more than enhance the confusion, while Eysenck (1970) discusses such analyses. Lurie (1937) factor analysed over 200 responses to the *Study of Values*, and obtained only four main factors. These were as follows:

1 social and altruistic
2 'philistine' (aggressive, go-getting, utilitarian, anti-cultural)
3 theoretical
4 religious.

No. 2 is a good example of the difficulty of naming factors.

Coates (1950) constructed a questionnaire to test the true statistical independence of these four factors, and his results confirmed those of Lurie.

Opinions differ as to the interpretation of these data. Allport feels that the point has been missed if his test is factor analysed. Eysenckians would argue, though, that data must not be ignored, and that Spranger's original typology was conducted from the armchair. They would therefore see the factor analyses as an advance.

A very widely observed result is the high correlation between scores on the SVIB and the Study of Values (Eysenck, 1970). The closeness is not sufficient for the tests to be used interchangeably, but it is extremely interesting to find so close an empirical relation between interests and values. Tyler (1967) goes so far as to speculate whether the tests are measuring the same things (it is always possible that a correlation between two variables x and y is determined by their joint causal dependence on a third variable z). In this case we can only add to the speculations. But it seems fair to guess that both values and interests are determined by a fundamental orientation to the world, jointly acting with an individual's orectic personality. Eysenck has linked interests with attitudes, and one could also regard values as attitudes (see B3). Eysenck believes that the fundamental dimensions of social attitudes have now been found, but admits that a considerable amount more has to be done on interests and values. Apart from establishing decisively the fundamental dimensions, *causal* theories need to be put forward, of the kind used in connexion with crime, political persuasion, and the like. Also it would be helpful to fit values and interests into the hierarchical scheme for the *structure of personality* which Eysenck uses for extraversion-introversion, and extends thus to the realm of attitudes:

Ideology level
Attitude level
Habitual level
Specific opinion level

19
Roles and social behaviour

It is frequently urged to psychologists that if their task is to predict behaviour, they had better turn to the social sciences. Nearly seventy years ago, in 1908, the first two books to bear the title 'Social Psychology' were published. One was written by William McDougall, a psychologist, and it stressed the *intra*-personal determinants of behaviour. In other words, it contended that individual differences in social performance were caused by differences within the individuals. The other, by Ross, a sociologist, stressed the *inter*-personal determinants of behaviour. This debate between sociology and psychology has continued ever since.

How do individual differences affect behaviour?
Cattell, as we have told (see p. 48), sees his task as the prediction of human behaviour. Therefore he is compelled to include in his 'specification equation' the variables which cannot be included under the heading of 'stable individual difference'. These variables include mood, role, and situation. Cattell has recorded his intention of classifying situations, but we know of no data on this. In the meantime his equation is stimulating but impractical, though it shows how data could be gathered. Some data have been gathered, and it can be used to choose between some of the theoretical positions which have

been adopted.

If the task is the prediction of human behaviour, one finds many experts crowding forward to state their views. Speaking broadly, the sociologist asserts that human behaviour – all of it – is determined by culture, socialization, and roles (see B2). In this view, individuality is either totally ignored, or dismissed as being irrelevant to the prediction of behaviour. A typical example is the position of Gerth and Mills (1953), in a book called *Character and Social Structure*. They flatly state: 'The person is composed of the roles he enacts.' One wonders what is left when the person stops acting. Some psychologists, on the other hand, adopt the opposite position – that all behaviour is determined by intra-personal traits. Perhaps Eysenck has neglected the role of situation a little here. However, both extreme positions have been rendered obsolete by recent work in personality theory and social psychology.

Michael Argyle and Brian Little (1972), in an admirable paper, bring the issue down to a precise question: 'Do personality traits apply to social behaviour?' Argyle and Little specify a number of different theoretical positions which might be adopted in response to their question. As an example, consider three individuals acting in situations in which their assertiveness may be measured. Their behaviour may vary in four ways. The first of these is called *total person variability*. The three individuals would each have a unique score in the first situation, and this would be unchanging for the other two situations. For example, if we assume that the three persons behaved differently because of their extraversion, it could be alleged that extraversion had been shown to be perfectly consistent, and trans-situationally stable. Argyle and Little, incidentally, regard this as a 'most extreme' view, and they do not actually impute it to any theorist. That is as well, for there is good reason to doubt the feasibility of such a position. Mischel (1968, 1969) has reviewed literature of this kind, and has argued that traits are more usefully regarded as products of the perceiver's categorizing behaviour than as attributes of the perceived.

The second theoretical position discussed by Argyle and Little is called *total situation variability*. According to such a position, the three individuals would always score the same as each other, but their joint scores would vary with each situation. This view is associated with sociology, and would most readily be applicable in crowd situations (this is not at all far-fetched, as is apparent from attending a football match, to say nothing of party political rallies or demonstrations).

The third position is called *dispositional*. In this the individuals will differ from each other in every situation, but their rank order will remain the same. Thus both persons and situations contribute to the performance of the behaviour.

The fourth and last position is called *interaction*. The 'interaction' concept is the same as that which is used in the analysis of variance. That is, both the principal variables – persons and situations – contribute to the outcome, but in a trans-summative way; that is, each person changes his score on each situation, but the rank order of persons is not necessarily maintained over different situations.

Argyle and Little do not present these as definite hypotheses, but rather as food for thought. One obvious point which they do not bring out is that the positions each seem to apply to at least *some* social behaviours. A second point is that they are concerned with behavioural variance contributed by *persons*: not by a particular trait but by the total personality.

The above are the relatively abstract ways of considering possible relationships between personality and behaviour in social settings. Argyle and Little regard them as only preliminary to the interpretation of the variability of the behaviour; and they mention several common interpretations. 'Total person variability' is sometimes implied by those theorists who stress a conception of personality as constant patterns of behaviour, such as Eysenck. 'Total situation variability' is most commonly postulated by role theorists. 'Dispositional' behaviour is emphasized by those who conceive of traits as a disposition to respond in certain ways to certain situations: Cattell is the obvious example here.

It is possible, of course, to hold that all or some of the positions are applicable for some behaviours, and some theories would seem to imply this. Kelly (1955) and Bannister

(1966, etc.), in considering personality as a personal construct system (see Chapter 6), may be said to consider that both the person and the situation are important determiners of behaviour. 'Social behaviour theory' (Mischel, 1968), on the other hand, applies to no particular position: it regards personality as a set of S–R links: that is, of response patterns applied to particular situations (see B1). Although uncommitted in terms of the dimensions raised by Argyle and Little, it could be put in the family of 'total situation variability'.

This completes the primary theoretical considerations. We may now turn to the evidence, although along with Argyle and Little 'we shall see there is considerable latitude for alternative interpretations of the same empirical data'.

Evidence concerning personality traits and social behaviour
Two types of investigation have been used: those which yield a correlation between different situations for a single person on a single trait; and those in which groups of persons are studied, and the variance is partitioned between persons, situations, and the interaction between them.

For example, *leadership* was once thought of as a trait, but Gibb (1969) and Hollander and Willis (1967) found that situational variance exceeded person variance on tasks pertaining to leadership. It seems that the emergence of leaders is a function of the group *task* as well as of the properties of the members. *Persuasibility* has similarly been found to be a complex function of personality, the source, the message, etc. (McGuire, 1969, concluded that it is not possible to ascribe persuasibility in general to individuals). Mischel (1968) summarized a considerable body of evidence, and concluded that cross-situational generality did hold for variables such as intelligence, field dependence (see p. 99) and reaction time, but did *not* hold for conditionability, dependence, attitudes to authority, rigidity, and moral behaviour. It is for this reason that Mischel propounded *social* behaviour theory as an alternative to personality theory *in the realm of social behaviour*.

A good deal of information has been gathered from questionnaire studies, but Argyle and Little distrust this; for, they allege, it has not been shown to be indicative of social *behaviour*, whatever it might imply for *dispositions*. Moreover, they allege that even data with apparently reliable perceptions of traits by judges, may be untrustworthy. They cite a study of Mulaik (1964), who factor analysed ratings by judges of (a) real persons, (b) stereotyped persons, and (c) the meanings of trait words. He found that there was high factor similarity across these domains, and inferred that personality factors *in the judge* might be responsible for the imputation of traits to the judged persons.

A more reliable source is the set of studies which examine the variance to allocate its origin to persons, situations, or their interaction. Endler, Hunt and Rosenstein (1962) presented subjects with an inventory, in which they recorded their probable anxiety reactions to a set of situations. To the great surprise of all concerned, the variance from persons contributed approximately 5 per cent; but so did the variance from situations. It was the interaction variance which was largest. With this result, the authors declared that as far as anxiousness was concerned, the 'persons-situations' debate was meaningless, or at least wrongly put: for some people some situations caused anxiety, and for other people, other situations did.

Several other studies reviewed by Argyle and Little made similar findings, which leads them to conclude that the 'persons or situations' problem was too simply posed. When the interaction variance is added to the possible sources of variance, it is a soluble problem. And for at least some social variables, the interaction variance exceeds that of either persons or situations alone. Also, with the passage of time and in more adequately functioning groups, situations are relatively more important sources of variation than are persons. The authors shrewdly note that for many measures of individual differences in social behaviour it would be prudent to include situational variables. Without them, the maximum *possible* validity coefficient would be (say) 0·5, if the maximum persons variance was 25 per cent.

Argyle and Little report a similar study of their own, in which persons accounted for only 16 per cent of the data, and they add this to the data which can be brought to bear on the theoretical positions sketched at the outset.

The authors conclude that the idea of personality as consistent patterns of behaviour received very little support, at least as regards *social* behaviour. Nor can personality be considered as dispositions to respond, for this would predict that all variance would be due either to persons or situations; whereas several studies found an interaction of forty per cent or higher. Social behaviour theory (which for these purposes can be regarded as the same as 'role theory') predicts low variance for persons, and is thus supported; but it also predicts maximum variance for situations, and here is unsupported.

Theoretical conclusions

None of the models considered by Argyle and Little was adequate to predict much of the data. We feel that this is because they were conceptualized as exclusive types. Behaviour, being no respecter of our models, is more complex. At the very least it seems obvious that some of the models apply to some types of situations and persons, and others to others. We do not have enough data to say. Several sorts of information are lacking. First, it is obvious that we need to test many more persons, in many more situations, on many more social tasks. But in order to do this as economically as possible, it is necessary, secondly, to attempt some sort of classification of situations and social behaviours. To try to classify persons would perhaps be to beg the question which we are trying to answer. However, a classification of situations is possible, and several authors have worked on it, or report work in progress. Cattell (1965, etc.) and Frederiksen (1972) make a plea for a taxonomy of situations. However, from a very different quarter there comes a set of hard data which are most welcome. The party responsible is R. G. Barker, who, together with colleagues, has been working as a sociologist-biologist-psychologist in a field founded by himself: *psychological ecology*, or the naturalistic study of human beings in their environment. For psychologists who see their task as predicting behaviour, as much of it as possible, Barker's work is salutary.

The classic example is Barker and Wright (1955), a study which contributes to personality theory, role theory, and the analysis of situations. Barker and Wright set themselves to study the behavioural life of a small town in Kansas. They concluded that there were *800* distinct public situations. And these situations had rigidly bound sets of rules, which are equivalent to role-expectations for individuals. As they put it: 'When we are in church we behave church, when we are in school we behave school.' And the best way of *predicting what a person will do* is not to ask about his personality, but about the rules governing the situation (see B2).

20
Anti-conclusions

Selectivity

In the course of a short text we have ranged widely, introducing many of the problems, and some of the data, involved in the question of 'individual differences'. While we have included our own comments, we have not attempted any final evaluation. We have not even tried to integrate the various aspects. This is partly because this is specifically an *introduction*; we hope to raise questions for the reader rather than settle them. It is also because we think that it would be misleading to suggest that unity exists in this area. 'Individual differences', like psychology itself, is a heterogeneous collection of investigations and theories, which originate in varying assumptions and serve varying purposes.

We are aware that we have been selective; but not, we hope, partial. American readers, if such there be, may think we have unduly favoured British work: of our five featured personalities, four are British, one American.

But this, we think, reflects a real difference in the traditions, and perhaps the values of the countries.

Another reason that there is no overall assessment is that your authors do not agree. It is not so much that one is arguing for black, and the other for white. Rather, RK has a particular point of view which he wishes to propagate, while

JR's attitude is compounded more of doubts and puzzlement.

Following the plan described in the Preface, it falls to JR to write these words. Thus there is a danger that RK's opinions will be distorted (as they will certainly be shortened). However we shall start with them.

One author's views

RK begins by arguing that differential psychology is pre-eminent among psychological issues, since if psychology is to be a general science, with generalizing laws, it must somehow deal with the problem of individuals. However, differential psychology also raises problems of its own: logical, methodological, and empirical. These fall into two groups. The first group is concerned with the nature and extent of human differences. Logically, these are infinite, or at any rate capable of being classified in an infinite number of ways. However, in practice, there is good reason to suppose that a person's individuality, considered as the greater part of the variance of his likely behaviour and experience, can be pinned down by a complex of personality measures. On this basis, drawing on the work of Allport, Eysenck, and Cattell, it would be possible to create a science of individual persons or *idiography*: a scientific version of biography, coupling the depth and richness of the latter with the mathematical precision of personality tests.

Another of this group of problems concerns the nature of psychology itself. Conceived as the science of behaviour and experience, psychology deals, it seems, not only with the past behaviour of man but also his future. In order to predict this, psychology must characterize the essential determining agents in man's nature, and thus understand human potential.

One aspect of this is the rapidly increasing technical ability that human beings have to alter themselves. Some mental capacities can be multiplied by the use of computers. Parts of the body can be replaced, with results sometimes better than the original. Direct stimulation of the brain, and biofeedback (see A2) likewise point to the possibility of an individual *controlling himself* in a way hardly thought of until now. More

134

important, however, is the fact that man consists of an embodied brain. The essential fact about man, however, that in which his humanity essentially consists, is his consciousness. This has been thought to be inextricably tied to the physical arrangements: but there is no logical reason why this should be so. It is possible to imagine that man may encounter, or create, or himself become, pure mentality. Such suppositions are to be found in many works of speculative fiction, for example those of Olaf Stapledon and Arthur C. Clarke. The importance of such work is that it serves the purpose of originating scientific conjectures and subjecting them to imaginary experimental manipulation. Since psychology as yet allows no place for such speculation, the ideas necessarily overflow into literature.

The postulation of disembodied intelligence raises the unsolved body-mind problem (see A1, A2, F1, F7). While this remains a mystery, we can at least say that there is no reason to think that evolution is at an end. Moreover as the genetic code, and the role of environment, begin to be understood, it is possible to envisage the deliberate alteration of the human race in whatever direction is desired.

The second group of problems are those concerning the self. The puzzle here is whether there is really some transcendent self, independent of states of the brain and the body, as many religions teach; or whether what we call the self is merely a fleeting sensation of individuality subsisting momentarily in successive components of consciousness as David Hume and, later, William James asserted. Perhaps only future research will solve this. It is impossible to tell whether the successful research will be philosophical, psychological, or physiological.

However it should be possible to attain a much clearer concept of the self by inquiring how the concept is actually used by people, and in what ways an awareness of self enters into everyday life and decisions. A start on this has been made already by therapists such as Rogers.

As far as our present knowledge extends, it must be concluded that we cannot, logically, say whether it is much or little. We cannot assess the advance of science in terms of its nearness to completion, since we can never say how far off this is. All we can do is set up sub-goals, as it were, in the light of particular needs of the human race at any one time. Indeed the concept of 'pure research' apart from values is a fallacious one. Following Nicholas Maxwell (1970, 1974) it is argued that science is not engaged in seeking 'the truth' but beautiful and elegant knowledge. As far as psychologists are concerned, their task is not merely to collect facts about man, but to liberate him, and to inculcate in him a spirit of delight, compassion, and love.

The other author's views

For his part, JR agrees with some of this. He agrees, for example, that we can learn something interesting by looking at science fiction. But he wishes to suggest (and has done so for example in *Science Fiction Monthly* and *New Behaviour*) that one thing such writing does is *reflect* the ways we are thinking about ourselves. In this respect science fiction is analogous to myth in pre-literate societies. There is less reason to think that from its divergent thought we can *predict* what the future will hold. It may be suggested, too, that *part* of what psychology is doing is finding new, more acceptable ways of thinking about ourselves. If one considers a theory such as that of Freud, the influence of which is undeniable, one must be struck by the equivocal nature of the evidence for it and against it. Critics such as Eysenck dismiss it out of hand on the grounds of untestability. Yet it seems clear that human behaviour is considered differently now as compared to a hundred years ago, and that this is at least partly due to the acceptance of concepts (such as unconscious motivation, or the role of early experiences) formulated, if they were not originated, by Freud. The reasons for this need to be elucidated by a social historian. To at least some extent a similar argument can be applied to the study of individual differences. Thus, following Galton, it is confidently asserted that intelligence is normally distributed. Yet intelligence is measured by instruments specifically constructed so as to yield a normal symmetrical curve.

Again, it does not follow that because measurement is possible, people must be treated differently in accordance with their scores. For example, facilities for sport are not restricted to those children who show a special aptitude for it. It might be said that comprehensive schooling has recently been developed to overcome just this objection. A glance at other cultures must show, however, that the comprehensive system is just one further selection from an infinite range of possibilities. Psychologists and non-psychologists alike should beware of thinking that decisions really based upon politics, emotion, or personal ambition are scientific in nature.

This is not to say, however, that nothing is known. The uncomfortable truth is that things are not black and white. We do know a great deal more about human behaviour, at least in some areas and in our own culture, than we did in say 1850. And we know it through a new means, namely the application of techniques of experiment and statistical analysis. This is illustrated through much of the present series, and as far as individual differences are concerned, in the present text. Individual behaviour, it can be claimed, is understood, not just looked at differently, in a way that was not formerly possible. Psychology contributes something not contributed by literature, religion, or magic. Karl Popper has made a distinction between prediction, which is the aim of science, and prophecy, which is offered by magic. R. S. Peters (1953), taking this point, argues that psychologists should not be criticized because they cannot say what a given child will become or whether a statesman will break a promise. As he puts it, physicists are not expected to predict whether the 12.30 to Liverpool Street will be five minutes late. Astronomy is almost alone among the sciences in making such long-term unconditional predictions. Astrology, of course, claims to do so with respect to human behaviour, but following the extensive researches of Gauquelin (1970) we can say fairly conclusively that the claim is false. However, as we argued right at the start, it is precisely the individual case that is our problem. We have not solved it, but both here and in D1 have tried to set out some of the issues.

137

In psychological issues it is almost impossible to disentangle the scientific, practical, ethical, political, and many other aspects. This is much more of a problem than it is even for other kinds of inquiry. It is not just a question of whether or not to work on, say, nerve gas – a perplexing but relatively straightforward issue of conscience such as a biologist might face. It is that *any* psychological investigation must interact with people in incalculable ways. It must derive from, and in turn contribute to, our conception of ourselves and the ways we treat each other. (This might seem somewhat grandiose when applied to short-term memory (see A6) or the Müller–Lyer illusion (see A4); but in the science fictional mirror we often glimpse alternative futures triggered by some seemingly minor event in the past.)

Psychology, as represented in the present series, is one of a group of inquiries which have emerged as systematic disciplines quite recently. Psychology is discriminable by its focus on certain sets of problems and its emphasis on certain sorts of method (especially those of experiment). As a whole, what these inquiries seem to give is a new perspective from which the human race can regard itself; one not available to even the most profound and subtle thinkers of the past. Part of what this entails is indeed the ability to make deliberate choices. But far from showing what these choices should be, this new perspective presents a complexity more baffling than ever before.

As to its being the task of psychology to enhance man's capacity for pleasant emotions, or what not, this seems to end up more or less a matter of personal opinion. On equally personal grounds it can be argued that in human variety there lies value and some safeguard for future development. Since the future is logically and practically unpredictable, let us at least keep open as many options as possible.

Selected References and Name Index

The numbers in italics after each entry refer to page numbers within this book. Those in brackets indicate references to the author, or subject of a biography, but not to the particular book or article cited.

Allport, G. W. (1961) *Pattern and Growth in Personality.* New York: Holt, Rinehart & Winston. *19, 124 (19, 27, 44–5, 52–3, 100, 115–18, 134)*

Allport, G. W., Vernon, P. E. and Lindzey, G. (1951) *A Study of Values.* Boston, Mass.: Houghton Mifflin. *123–5*

Anastasi, A. (1958) *Differential Psychology.* (3rd edn) New York: Macmillan. *81, 93, 105–6*

Argyle, M. and Little, B. (1972) Do personality traits apply to social behaviour? *Journal of the Theory of Social Behaviour 2* (1): 1–35. *127–31*

Bannister, D. and Fransella, F. (1971) *Inquiring Man.* Harmondsworth: Penguin. *28, 56, 128–9*

Barker, R. G. and Wright, H. F. (1955) *Midwest and its Children.* New York: Harper. *131–2*

Burt, C. (1938) *The Young Delinquent.* University of London Press. *61 (13, 31, 33, 38–9, 49, 60, 75–8)*

Burt, C. (1949) The structure of the mind: A review of the results of factor analysis. *British Journal of Educational Psychology 19:* 100–14, 176–99. *63–4*

Burt, C. (1966) The genetic determination of differences in intelligence. *British Journal of Psychology 57:* 137–53. *84–5*

Butcher, H. J. (1968) *Human Intelligence: Its Nature and Assessment*. London: Methuen. *64*

Cattell, R. B. (1965) *The Scientific Study of Personality*. Harmondsworth: Penguin. *55, 85, 126, 131 (13, 38, 48–51, 122, 134)*

Cole, M., Gay, J., Glick, J. A. and Sharp, D. W. (1971) *The Cultural Context of Learning and Thinking*. London: Methuen. *111–12*

Deakin, M. (1973) *The Children on the Hill*. London: Quartet. *99, 113*

Eysenck, H. J. (1966) Personality and experimental psychology. *Bulletin of the British Psychological Society 19* (62): 1–28. *17 (11–14, 38–40, 49, 66, 78, 92, 97, 134)*

Eysenck, H. J. (1970) *The Structure of the Human Personality*. (3rd edn) London: Methuen. *122, 124–5*

Eysenck, H. J. (1971) *Race, Intelligence and Education*. London: Maurice Temple-Smith. *89–91*

Galton, F. (1869) *Hereditary Genius*. London: Macmillan (also Fontana, 1962). *25, 50, 67 (13, 20, 23–6, 30–1, 59, 75–7, 79, 81, 83–5)*

Galton, F. (1893) *Inquiries into Human Faculty and its Development*. London: Macmillan (also Everyman, 1907). *21, 26*

Ghiselin, B. (1952) *The Creative Process*. Berkeley, Calif.: University of California Press. *71*

Guilford, J. P. (1950) Creativity. *American Psychologist 5*: 444–54. *67–8 (38–9, 122)*

Guilford, J. P. (1967) *The Nature of Human Intelligence*. New York: McGraw-Hill. *62–3*

Hudson, L. (1968) *Frames of Mind: Ability, Perception and Self-Perception in the Arts and Sciences*. London: Methuen. *66, 69–70 (47)*

Jensen, A. R. (1969a) How much can we boost IQ and scholastic achievement? *Harvard Educational Review 39*: 1–123. *90 (42)*

Jensen, A. R. (1969b) Reducing the heredity-environment uncertainty. *Harvard Educational Review 39*: 209–43. *90*

Kitto, H. D. F. (1955) *The Greeks*. Harmondsworth: Penguin. *100*

Leach, E. (1970) *Lévi-Strauss*. London: Collins/Fontana. *(38)*

Magee, B. (1973) *Popper*. London: Collins/Fontana. *17 (13, 27, 29–30)*

140

Mischel, W. (1968) *Personality and Assessment*. New York: Wiley. *127, 129*

Price-Williams, D. R. (ed.) (1969) *Cross-Cultural Studies*. Harmondsworth: Penguin.

Radford, J. and Burton, A. (1974) *Thinking: Its Nature and Development*. London: Wiley. *65, 74, 109*

Richardson, K. and Spears, D. (eds) (1972) *Race, Culture and Intelligence*. Harmondsworth: Penguin.

Shuey, A. M. (1966) *The Testing of Negro Intelligence*. (2nd edn) New York: Social Science Press. *90–2*

Stapledon, O. (1930) *Last and First Men*. London: Methuen (also Penguin, 1963). *135*

Strong, E. K. (1953) *Vocational Interests of Men and Women*. California: Stanford University Press. *120–2*

Taylor, C. W. and Barron, F. (1963) *Scientific Creativity*. New York: Wiley. *73*

Vernon, P. E. (1950) *The Structure of Human Abilities*. London: Methuen. *63 (13, 38)*

Vernon, P. E. (1964) *Personality Assessment*. London: Methuen. *69*

Vernon, P. E. (1969) *Intelligence and Cultural Environment*. London: Methuen. *65, 109*

Wiseman, S. (ed.) (1967) *Intelligence and Ability*. Harmondsworth: Penguin.

Subject Index